Life of Th

Henry Hart Milman

Alpha Editions

This edition published in 2022

ISBN : 9789356899490

Design and Setting By
Alpha Editions
www.alphaedis.com
Email - info@alphaedis.com

EDITOR'S PREFACE.

PERHAPS the chapter of English history fullest of romantic interest, is that containing the life of Thomas à Becket. In fact, the great struggle between Becket and Henry II.,—between individual genius and sovereign power, between a subject and his king, between religion and the sword, between the Church and the State, is scarcely equaled in the annals of the world. And nowhere do we find a parallel to the strange story of Becket's life, beginning in Oriental legend, ending in heroic tragedy. By an accident of position, he questioned with the terrible power of genius the divine right of kings, and the grateful people of England, a hundred thousand at a time, flocked as pilgrims to his tomb.

The biography here presented has been taken from Dean Milman's great history of Latin Christianity. The style is at once dignified, terse, and eloquent. The learning of Milman is abundant and accurate, his judgment singularly sound and free from prejudice. One of the gems of his history is this life of Becket. A biography of the biographer is part of our plan, and we gladly transfer to our pages, from the English Cyclopedia, a sketch of Milman's life.

*****

The Rev. HENRY HART MILMAN, D.D., Dean of St. Paul's Cathedral, was born February 10th, 1791, in London. He is the youngest son of Sir Francis Milman, first baronet, who was physician to George III., and is brother to Sir William George Milman. He was educated at Dr. Burney's academy at Greenwich, at Eton College, and at Brazenose College, Oxford, where he took his degrees of B. A. and M. A., and of which he was elected a Fellow. In 1812 he received the Newdegate prize for his English poem on the Apollo Belvidere. In 1815 he published "Fazio, a Tragedy," which was performed with success at Covent Garden Theatre, at a period when theatrical managers seized upon a published play, and produced it without an author's consent. Mr. Milman could not even enforce the proper pronunciation of the name of "Fazio." He took holy orders in 1817, and was appointed vicar of St. Mary's, Reading. In the early part of 1818 he published "Samor, Lord of the Bright City, an Heroic Poem," of which a second edition was called for in the course of the same year. The hero of this poem is a personage of the legendary history of Britain in the early part of the Saxon invasions of England. The fullest account of his exploits is given in Dugdale's "Baronage," under his title of Earl of Gloucester. Harrison, in the "Description of Britain," prefixed to Holinshed's "Chronicle," calls him Eldulph de Samor. The Bright City is Gloucester,

(Caer Gloew in British.) In 1820 Mr Milman published "The Fall of Jerusalem," a dramatic poem founded on Josephus's narrative of the siege of the sacred city. This, in some respects his most beautiful poem, established his reputation. In 1821, he was elected Professor of Poetry in the University of Oxford, and published three other dramatic poems, "The Martyr of Antioch," "Balshazzar," and "Anne Boleyn." In 1827 he published sermons at the "Bampton Lecture," 8vo., and in 1829, without his name, "The History of the Jews," 3 vols. 18vo. A collected edition of his "Poetical Works," was published in 1840, which, besides the works above mentioned, and his smaller poems, contains the "Nala and Damayanti," translated from the Sanskrit. In the same year he published his "History of Christianity from the Birth of Christ, to the Abolition of Paganism in the Roman Empire," 3 vols. 8vo., in which he professes to view Christianity as a historian, in its moral, social, and political influences, referring to its doctrines no further than is necessary for explaining the general effect of the system. It is the work of an accomplished and liberal-minded scholar. At the commencement of 1849 appeared "The Works of Quintus Horatius Flaccus, illustrated chiefly from the Remains of Ancient Art, with a Life by the Rev. H. H. Milman," 8vo., a beautiful and luxurious edition. Mr. Milman's Life of Horace, and critical remarks on the merits of the Roman poet, are written with much elegance of style, and are very interesting.

In November 1849, Mr. Milman, who had for some years been Rector of St. Margaret's, Westminster, and a Canon of Westminster, was made Dean of St. Paul's. Dean Milman's latest publication is a "History of Latin Christianity, including that of the Popes to the Pontificate of Nicholas V.," 3 vols. 8vo. 1854. This work is a continuation of the author's "History of Christianity," and yet is in itself a complete work. To give it that completeness he has gone over the history of Christianity in Rome during the first four centuries. The author states that he is occupied with the continuation of the history down to the close of the pontificate of Nicholas V., that is, to 1455.[1] Besides the works before mentioned, Dean Milman is understood to have contributed numerous articles to the "Quarterly Review;" and his edition of Gibbon's "Decline and Fall of the Roman Empire," presented the great historian with more ample illustrations than he had before received. This edition has been republished, with additional notes and verifications, by Dr. W. Smith.

Dean Milman is destined to become a household word in historical literature, and we are glad to present the many with this favorable specimen of his work.

May, 1859.

O. W. Wight.

LIFE OF THOMAS À BECKET.

Legend.

POPULAR poetry, after the sanctification of Becket, delighted in throwing the rich colors of marvel over his birth and parentage. It invented, or rather interwove with the pedigree of the martyr, one of those romantic traditions which grew out of the wild adventures of the crusades, and which occur in various forms in the ballads of all nations. That so great a saint should be the son of a gallant champion of the cross, and of a Saracen princess, was a fiction too attractive not to win general acceptance. The father of Becket, so runs the legend, a gallant soldier, was a captive in the Holy Land, and inspired the daughter of his master with an ardent attachment. Through her means he made his escape; but the enamored princess could not endure life without him. She too fled and made her way to Europe. She had learned but two words of the Christian language, London and Gilbert. With these two magic sounds upon her lips she reached London; and as she wandered through the streets, constantly repeating the name of Gilbert, she was met by Becket's faithful servant. Becket, as a good Christian, seems to have entertained religious scruples as to the propriety of wedding the faithful, but misbelieving, or, it might be, not sincerely believing maiden. The case was submitted to the highest authority, and argued before the Bishop of London. The issue was the baptism of the princess, by the name of Matilda (that of the empress queen,) and their marriage in St. Paul's, with the utmost publicity and splendor.

But of this wondrous tale, not one word had reached the ears of any of the seven or eight contemporary biographers of Becket, most of them his most intimate friends or his most faithful attendants.[2] It was neither known to John of Salisbury, his confidential adviser and correspondent, nor to Fitz-Stephen, an officer of his court in chancery, and dean of his chapel when archbishop, who was with him at Northampton, and at his death; nor to Herbert de Bosham, likewise one of his officers when chancellor, and his faithful attendant throughout his exile; nor to the monk of Pontigny, who waited upon him and enjoyed his most intimate confidence during his retreat in that convent; nor to Edward Grim, his standard-bearer, who on his way from Clarendon, reproached him with his weakness, and having been constantly attached to his person, finally interposed his arm between his master and the first blow of the assassin. Nor were these ardent admirers of Becket silent from any severe aversion to the marvelous; they relate, with unsuspecting faith, dreams and prognostics which revealed to the mother the future greatness of her son, even his elevation to the see of Canterbury.[3]

To the Saxon descent of Becket, a theory in which, on the authority of an eloquent French writer,[4] modern history has seemed disposed to acquiesce, these biographers not merely give no support, but furnish direct contradiction. The lower people no doubt admired during his life, and worshiped after death, the blessed Thomas of Canterbury, and the people were mostly Saxon. But it was not as a Saxon, but as a Saint, that Becket was the object of unbounded popularity during his life, of idolatry after his death.

Parentage and education.

The father of Becket, according to the distinct words of one contemporary biographer, was a native of Rouen, his mother of Caen.[5] Gilbert was no knight-errant, but a sober merchant, tempted by commercial advantages to settle in London: his mother neither boasted of royal Saracenic blood, nor bore the royal name of Matilda: she was the daughter of an honest burgher of Caen. His Norman descent is still further confirmed by his claim of relationship, or connexion at least, as of common Norman descent, with Archbishop Theobald.[6] The parents of Becket, he asserts himself, were merchants of unimpeached character, not of the lowest class. Gilbert Becket is said to have served the honorable office of sheriff, but his fortune was injured by fires and other casualties.[7] |Born A. D. 1118.| The young Becket received his earliest education among the monks of Merton in Surrey, towards whom he cherished a fond attachment, and delighted to visit them in the days of his splendor. The dwelling of a respectable London merchant seems to have been a place where strangers of very different pursuits, who resorted to the metropolis of England, took up their lodging: and to Gilbert Becket's house came persons both disposed and qualified to cultivate in various ways the extraordinary talents displayed by the youth, who was singularly handsome, and of engaging manners.[8] A knight, whose name, Richard de Aquila, occurs with distinction in the annals of the time, one of his father's guests, delighted in initiating the gay and spirited boy in chivalrous exercises, and in the chase with hawk and hound. On a hawking adventure the young Becket narrowly escaped being drowned in the Thames. At the same time, or soon after, he was inured to business by acting as clerk to a wealthy relative, Osborn Octuomini, and in the office of the Sheriff of London.[9] His accomplishments were completed by a short residence in Paris, the best school for the language spoken by the Norman nobility. To his father's house came likewise two learned civilians from Bologna, no doubt on some mission to the Archbishop of Canterbury. They were so captivated by young Becket, that they strongly recommended him to Archbishop Theobald, whom the father of Becket reminded of their common honorable descent from a knightly family near the town of Thiersy.[10]

Becket was at once on the high road of advancement. |In the household

of the Archbishop.| His extraordinary abilities were cultivated by the wise patronage, and employed in the service of the primate. Once he accompanied that prelate to Rome;[11] and on more than one other occasion visited that great centre of Christian affairs. He was permitted to reside for a certain time at each of the great schools for the study of the canon law, Bologna and Auxerre.[12] He was not, however, without enemies. Even in the court of Theobald began the jealous rivalry with Roger, afterwards Archbishop of York, then Archdeacon of Canterbury.[13] Twice the superior influence of the archdeacon obtained his dismissal from the service of Theobald; twice he was reinstated by the good offices of Walter, Bishop of Rochester. At length the elevation of Roger to the see of York left the field open to Becket. He was appointed to the vacant archdeaconry, the richest benefice, after the bishoprics, in England. From that time he ruled without rival in the favor of the aged Theobald. Preferments were heaped upon him by the lavish bounty of his patron.[14] During his exile he was reproached with his ingratitude to the king, who had raised him from poverty. "Poverty!" he rejoined; "even then I held the archdeaconry of Canterbury, the provostship of Beverley, a great many churches, and several prebends."[15] The trial and the triumph of Becket's precocious abilities was a negotiation of the utmost difficulty with the court of Rome. The first object was to obtain the legatine power for Archbishop Theobald; the second tended, more than almost all measures, to secure the throne of England to the house of Plantagenet. Archbishop Theobald, with his clergy, had inclined to the cause of Matilda and her son; they had refused to officiate at the coronation of Eustace, son of King Stephen. Becket not merely obtained from Eugenius III. the full papal approbation of this refusal, but a condemnation of Stephen (whose title had before been sanctioned by Eugenius himself,) as a perjured usurper.[16]

Accession of Henry II. Dec. 19, 1154.

But on the accession of Henry II., the aged Archbishop began to tremble at his own work; serious apprehensions arose as to the disposition of the young king towards the Church. His connexion was but remote with the imperial family (though his mother had worn the imperial crown, and some imperial blood might flow in his veins); but the Empire was still the implacable adversary of the papal power. Even from his father he might have received an hereditary taint of hatred to the Church, for the Count of Anjou had on many occasions shown the utmost hostility to the Hierarchy, and had not scrupled to treat churchmen of the highest rank with unexampled cruelty. In proportion as it was important to retain a young sovereign of such vast dominions in allegiance to the Church, so was it alarming to look forward to his disobedience. The Archbishop was anxious to place near his person some one who might counteract this suspected perversity, and to prevent his young mind from being alienated from the clergy by fierce and lawless counselors. He had discerned not merely unrivaled abilities, but with prophetic sagacity, his Archdeacon's lofty and devoted churchmanship. Through the recommendation of the primate, Becket was raised to the dignity of chancellor,[17] an office which made him the second civil power in the realm, inasmuch as his seal was necessary to countersign all royal mandates. Nor was it without great ecclesiastical influence, as in the chancellor was the appointment of all the royal chaplains, and the custody of vacant bishoprics, abbacies, and benefices.[18]

Becket Chancellor.

But the Chancellor, who was yet, with all his great preferments, only in deacon's orders, might seem disdainfully to throw aside the habits, feelings, restraints of the churchman, and to aspire as to the plenitude of secular power, so to unprecedented secular magnificence.[19] Becket shone out in all the graces of an accomplished courtier, in the bearing and valor of a gallant knight; though at the same time he displayed the most consummate abilities for business, the promptitude, diligence, and prudence of a practiced statesman. The beauty of his person, the affability of his manners, the extraordinary acuteness of his senses,[20] his activity in all chivalrous exercises, made him the chosen companion of the king in his constant diversions, in the chase and in the mimic war, in all but his debaucheries. The king would willingly have lured the Chancellor into this companionship likewise; but the silence of his bitterest enemies, in confirmation of his own solemn protestations, may be admitted as conclusive testimonies to his unimpeached morals.[21] The power of Becket throughout the king's dominions equaled that of the king himself—he was king in all but name: the world, it was said, had never seen two friends so entirely of one mind.[22] The well-known anecdote best illustrates their intimate familiarity. As they rode through the streets of London on a bleak

Winter day they met a beggar in rags. "Would it not be charity," said the king, "to give that fellow a cloak, and cover him from the cold?" Becket assented; on which the king plucked the rich furred mantle from the shoulders of the struggling Chancellor and threw it, to the amazement and admiration of the bystanders, no doubt to the secret envy of the courtiers at this proof of Becket's favor, to the shivering beggar.[23]

But it was in the graver affairs of the realm that Henry derived still greater advantage from the wisdom and the conduct of the Chancellor.[24] To Becket's counsels his admiring biographers attribute the pacification of the kingdom, the expulsion of the foreign mercenaries who during the civil wars of Stephen's reign had devastated the land and had settled down as conquerors, especially in Kent, the humiliation of the refractory barons and the demolition of their castles. The peace was so profound that merchants could travel everywhere in safety, and even the Jews collect their debts.[25] The magnificence of Becket redounded to the glory of his sovereign. In his ordinary life he was sumptuous beyond precedent; he kept an open table, where those who were not so fortunate as to secure a seat at the board had clean rushes strewn on the floor, on which they might repose, eat, and carouse at the Chancellor's expense. His household was on a scale vast even for that age of unbounded retainership, and the haughtiest Norman nobles were proud to see their sons brought up in the family of the merchant's son. |Ambassador to Paris A. D. 1160.| In his embassy to Paris to demand the hand of the Princess Margaret for the king's infant son, described with such minute accuracy by Fitz-Stephen,[26] he outshone himself, yet might seem to have a loyal rather than a personal aim in this unrivaled pomp. The French crowded from all quarters to see the splendid procession pass, and exclaimed, "What must be the king, whose Chancellor can indulge in such enormous expenditure?"

War in Toulouse.

Even in war the Chancellor had displayed not only the abilities of a general, but a personal prowess, which, though it found many precedents in those times, might appear somewhat incongruous in an ecclesiastic, who yet held all his clerical benefices. In the expedition made by King Henry to assert his right to the dominions of the Counts of Toulouse, Becket appeared at the head of seven hundred knights who did him service, and foremost in every adventurous exploit was the valiant Chancellor. Becket's bold counsel urged the immediate storming of the city, which would have been followed by the captivity of the King of France. Henry, in whose character impetuosity was strangely molded up with irresolution, dared not risk this violation of feudal allegiance, the captivity of his suzerain. The event of the war showed the policy as well as the superior military judgment of the warlike Chancellor. At a period somewhat later, Becket, who was left to reduce certain castles which held out against his master, unhorsed in single combat and took prisoner a knight of great distinction, Engelran de Trie. He returned to Henry in Normandy at the head of 1200 knights and 4000 stipendiary horsemen, raised and maintained at his own charge. If indeed there were grave churchmen even in those days who were revolted by these achievements in an ecclesiastic (he was still only in deacon's orders), the sentiment was by no means universal, nor even dominant. With some his valor and military skill only excited more ardent admiration. One of his biographers bursts out into this extraordinary panegyric on the Archdeacon of Canterbury: "Who can recount the carnage, the desolation, which he made at the head of a strong body of soldiers? He attacked castles, razed towns and cities to the ground, burned down houses and farms without a touch of pity, and never showed the slightest mercy to any one who rose in insurrection against his master's authority."[27]

Wealth of Becket.

The services of Becket were not unrewarded; the love and gratitude of his sovereign showered honors and emoluments upon him. Among his grants were the wardenship of the Tower of London, the lordship of the castle of Berkhampstead and the honor of Eye, with the service of a hundred and forty knights. Yet there must have been other and more prolific sources of his wealth, so lavishly displayed. Through his hands as Chancellor passed almost all grants and royal favors. He was the guardian of all escheated baronies and of all vacant benefices. It is said in his praise that he did not permit the king, as was common, to prolong those vacancies for his own advantage, that they were filled up with as much speed as possible; but it should seem, by subsequent occurrences, that no very strict account was kept of the king's monies spent by the Chancellor in the king's service and those expended by the Chancellor himself. This seems intimated by the care which he took to secure a general quittance from the chief justiciary of the realm before his elevation to the archbishopric.

But if in his personal habits and occupations Becket lost in some degree the churchman in the secular dignitary, was he mindful of the solemn trust imposed upon him by his patron the archbishop, and true to the interests of his order? Did he connive at, or at least did he not resist, any invasion on ecclesiastical immunities, or, as they were called, the liberties of the clergy? did he hold their property absolutely sacred? It is clear that he consented to levy the scutage, raised on the whole realm, on ecclesiastical as well as secular property. All that his friend John of Salisbury can allege in his defence is, that he bitterly repented of having been the minister of this iniquity.[28] "If with Saul he persecuted the Church, with Paul he is prepared to die for the Church." But probably the worst effect of this conduct as regards King Henry was the encouragement of his fatal delusion that, as archbishop, Becket would be as submissive to his wishes in the affairs of the Church as had been the pliant Chancellor. It was the last and crowning mark of the royal confidence that Becket was intrusted with the education of the young Prince Henry, the heir to all the dominions of the king.

April, 1161.

Six years after the accession of Henry II. died Theobald Archbishop of Canterbury. On the character of his successor depended the peace of the realm, especially if Henry, as no doubt he did, already entertained designs of limiting the exorbitant power of the Church. Becket, ever at his right hand, could not but occur to the mind of the king. Nothing in his habits of life or conduct could impair the hope that in him the loyal, the devoted, it might seem unscrupulous subject, would predominate over the rigid churchman. With such a prime minister, attached by former benefits, it might seem by the warmest personal love, still more by this last proof of boundless confidence, to his person, and as holding the united offices of Chancellor and Primate, ruling supreme both in Church and State, the king could dread no resistance, or if there were resistance, could subdue it without difficulty.

Rumor had already designated Becket as the future primate. A churchman, the Prior of Leicester, on a visit to Becket, who was ill at Rouen, pointing to his apparel, said, "Is this a dress for an Archbishop of Canterbury?" Becket himself had not disguised his hopes and fears. "There are three poor priests in England, any one of whose elevation to the see of Canterbury I should wish rather than my own. I know the very heart of the king; if I should be promoted, I must forfeit his favor or that of God."[29]

The king did not suddenly declare his intentions. The see was vacant for above a year,[30] and the administration of the revenues must have been in the department of the Chancellor. At length as Becket, who had received a commission to return to England on other affairs of moment, took leave of his sovereign at Falaise, Henry hastily informed him that those affairs were not the main object of his mission to England—it was for his election to the vacant archbishopric. Becket remonstrated, but in vain; he openly warned, it is said, his royal master that as Primate he must choose between the favor of God and that of the king—he must prefer that of God.[31] In those days the interests of the clergy and of God were held inseparable. Henry no doubt thought this but the decent resistance of an ambitious prelate. The advice of Henry of Pisa, the Papal Legate, overcame the faint and lingering scruples of Becket: he passed to England with the king's recommendation, mandate it might be called, for his election.

All which to the king would designate Becket as the future Primate could not but excite the apprehensions of the more rigorous churchmen. The monks of Canterbury, with whom rested the formal election, alleged as an insuperable difficulty that Becket had never worn the monastic habit, as almost all his predecessors had done.[32] The suffragan bishops would no doubt secretly resist the advancement, over all their heads, of a man who, latterly at least, had been more of a soldier, a courtier, and a lay statesman. Nor could the prophetic sagacity of any but the wisest discern the latent churchmanship in the ambitious and inflexible heart of Becket. It is recorded on authority, which I do not believe doubtful as to its authenticity, but which is the impassioned statement of a declared enemy, that nothing but the arrival of the great justiciary, Richard de Luci, with the king's peremptory commands, and with personal menaces of proscription and exile against the more forward opponents, awed the refractory monks and prelates to submission.

Gilbert Foliot.

At Whitsuntide Thomas Becket received priest's orders, and was then consecrated Primate of England with great magnificence in the Abbey of Westminster. The see of London being vacant, the ceremony was performed by the once turbulent, now aged and peaceful, Henry of Winchester, the brother of King Stephen. One voice alone, that of Gilbert Foliot, Bishop of Hereford,[33] broke the apparent harmony by a bitter sarcasm—"The king has wrought a miracle; he has turned a soldier and a layman into an archbishop." Gilbert Foliot, from first to last the firm and unawed antagonist of Becket, is too important a personage to be passed lightly by.[34] This sally was attributed no doubt by some at the time, as it was the subject afterwards of many fierce taunts from Becket himself, and of lofty vindication by Foliot, to disappointed ambition, as though he himself aspired to the primacy. Nor was there an ecclesiastic in England who might entertain more just hopes of advancement. He was admitted to be a man of unimpeachable life, of austere habits, and great learning. He had been Abbot of Gloucester and then Bishop of Hereford. He was in correspondence with four successive Popes, Cœlestine II., Lucius II., Eugenius III., Alexander, and with a familiarity which implies a high estimation for ability and experience. He is interfering in matters remote from his diocese, and commending other bishops, Lincoln and Salisbury, to the favorable consideration of the Pontiff. All his letters reveal as imperious and conscientious a churchman as Becket himself, and in Becket's position Foliot might have resisted the king as inflexibly.[35] He was, in short, a bold and stirring ecclesiastic, who did not scruple to wield, as he had done in several instances, that last terrible weapon of the clergy which burst on his own head, excommunication.[36] It may be added that, notwithstanding his sarcasm, there was no open breach between him and Becket. The primate acquiesced in, if he did not promote, the advancement of Foliot to the see of London;[37] and during that period letters of courtesy which borders on adulation were interchanged at least with apparent sincerity.[38]

The king had indeed wrought a greater miracle than himself intended, or than Foliot thought possible. Becket became at once not merely a decent prelate, but an austere and mortified monk: he seemed determined to make up for his want of ascetic qualifications; to crowd a whole life of monkhood into a few years.[39] Under his canonical dress he wore a monk's frock, haircloth next his skin; his studies, his devotions, were long, regular, rigid. At the mass he was frequently melted into passionate tears. In his outward demeanor, indeed, though he submitted to private flagellation, and the most severe macerations, Becket was still the stately prelate: his food, though scanty to abstemiousness, was, as his constitution required, more delicate; his charities were boundless. Archbishop Theobald had doubled the usual amount of the primate's alms, Becket again doubled that; and every night in privacy, no doubt more ostentatious than the most public exhibition, with his own hands he washed the feet of thirteen beggars. His table was still hospitable and sumptuous, but instead of knights and nobles, he admitted only learned clerks, and especially the regulars, whom he courted with the most obsequious deference. For the sprightly conversation of former times were read grave books in the Latin of the Church.

But the change was not alone in his habits and mode of life. The King could not have reproved, he might have admired, the most punctilious regard for the decency and the dignity of the highest ecclesiastic in the realm. But the inflexible churchman began to betray himself in more unexpected acts. While still in France Henry was startled at receiving a peremptory resignation of the chancellorship, as inconsistent with the religious functions of the primate. This act was as it were a bill of divorce from all personal intimacy with the king, a dissolution of their old familiar and friendly intercourse. It was not merely that the holy and austere prelate withdrew from the unbecoming pleasures of the court, the chase, the banquet, the tournament, even the war; they were no more to meet at the council board, and the seat of judicature. It had been said that Becket was co-sovereign with the king, he now appeared (and there were not wanting secret and invidious enemies to suggest, and to inflame the suspicion) a rival sovereign.[40] The king, when Becket met him on his landing at Southampton, did not attempt to conceal his dissatisfaction; his reception of his old friend was cold.

It were unjust to human nature, to suppose that it did not cost Becket a violent struggle, a painful sacrifice, thus as it were to rend himself from the familiarity and friendship of his munificent benefactor. It was no doubt a severe sense of duty which crushed his natural affections, especially as vulgar ambition must have pointed out a more sure and safe way to power and fame. Such ambition would hardly have hesitated between the ruling all orders through the king, and the solitary and dangerous position of opposing so powerful a monarch to maintain the interests and secure the favor of one order alone.

Becket at Tours. May 19, 1163.

Henry was now fully occupied with the affairs of Wales. Becket, with the royal sanction, obeyed the summons of Pope Alexander to the Council of Tours. Becket had passed through part of France at the head of an army of his own raising, and under his command; he had passed a second time as representing the king; he was yet to pass as an exile. At Tours, where Pope Alexander now held his court, and presided over his council, Becket appeared at the head of all the Bishops of England, except those excused on account of age or infirmity. So great was his reputation, that the Pope sent out all the cardinals except those in attendance on his own person to escort the primate of England into the city. In the council at Tours not merely was the title of Alexander to the popedom avouched with perfect unanimity, but the rights and privileges of the clergy asserted with more than usual rigor and distinctness. Some canons, one especially which severely condemned all encroachments on the property of the Church, might seem framed almost with a view to the impending strife with England.

Beginning of strife.

That strife, so impetuous might seem the combatants to join issue, broke out, during the next year, in all its violence. Both parties, if they did not commence, were prepared for aggression. The first occasion of public collision was a dispute concerning the customary payment of the ancient Danegelt, of two shillings on every hide of land, to the sheriffs of the several counties. The king determined to transfer this payment to his own exchequer: he summoned an assembly at Woodstock, and declared his intentions. All were mute but Becket; the archbishop opposed the enrolment of the decree, on the ground that the tax was voluntary, not of right. "By the eyes of God," said Henry, his usual oath, "it shall be enrolled!" "By the same eyes, by which you swear," replied the prelate, "it shall never be levied on my lands while I live!"[41] On Becket's part, almost the first act of his primacy was to vindicate all the rights, and to resume all the property which had been usurped, or which he asserted to have been usurped, from his see.[42] It was not likely that, in the turbulent times just gone by, there would have been rigid respect for the inviolability of sacred property. The title of the Church was held to be indefeasible. Whatever had once belonged to the Church might be recovered at any time; and the ecclesiastical courts claimed the sole right of adjudication in such causes. The primate was thus at once plaintiff, judge, and carried into execution his own judgments. The lord of the manor of Eynsford in Kent, who held of the king, claimed the right of presentation to that benefice. Becket asserted the prerogative of the see of Canterbury. On the forcible ejectment of his nominee by the lord, William of Eynsford, Becket proceeded at once to a sentence of excommunication, without regard to Eynsford's feudal superior the king. |Claims of Becket.| The primate next demanded the castle of Tunbridge from the head of the powerful family of De Clare; though it had been held by De Clare, and it was asserted, received in exchange for a Norman Castle, since the time of William the Conqueror. The attack on De Clare might seem a defiance of the whole feudal nobility: a determination to despoil them of their conquests, or grants from the sovereign.

Immunities of the clergy.

The king, on his side, wisely chose the strongest and more popular ground of the immunities of the clergy from all temporal jurisdiction. He appeared as guardian of the public morals, as administrator of equal justice to all his subjects, as protector of the peace of the realm. Crimes of great atrocity, it is said, of great frequency, crimes such as robbery and homicide, crimes for which secular persons were hanged by scores and without mercy, were committed almost with impunity, or with punishment altogether inadequate to the offence by the clergy; and the sacred name of clerk, exempted not only bishops, abbots, and priests, but those of the lowest ecclesiastical rank from the civil power. It was the inalienable right of the clerk to be tried only in the court of his bishop; and as that court could not award capital punishment, the utmost penalties were flagellation, imprisonment, and degradation. It was only after degradation, and for a second offence (for the clergy strenuously insisted on the injustice of a second trial for the same act,)[43] that the meanest of the clerical body could be brought to the level of the most highborn layman. But to cede one tittle of these immunities, to surrender the sacred person of a clergyman, whatever his guilt, to the secular power, was treason to the sacerdotal order: it was giving up Christ (for the Redeemer was supposed actually to dwell in the clerk, though his hands might be stained with innocent blood) to be crucified by the heathen.[44] To mutilate the person of one in holy orders was directly contrary to the Scripture (for with convenient logic, while the clergy rejected the example of the Old Testament as to the equal liability of priest and Levite with the ordinary Jew to the sentence of the law, they alleged it on their own part as unanswerable.) It was inconceivable, that hands which had but now made God should be tied behind the back, like those of a common malefactor, or that his neck should be wrung on a gibbet, before whom kings had but now bowed in reverential homage.[45]

The enormity of the evil is acknowledged by Becket's most ardent partisans.[46] The king had credible information laid before him that some of the clergy were absolute devils in guilt, that their wickedness could not be repressed by the ordinary means of justice, and were daily growing worse.

Becket himself had protected some notorious and heinous offenders. A clerk of the diocese of Worcester had debauched a maiden and murdered her father. Becket ordered the man to be kept in prison, and refused to surrender him to the king's justice.[47] Another in London, guilty of stealing a silver goblet, was claimed as only amenable to the ecclesiastical court. Philip de Brois, a canon of Bedford, had been guilty of homicide. The cause was tried in the bishop's court; he was condemned to pay a fine to the kindred of the slain man. Some time after, Fitz-Peter, the king's justiciary, whether from private enmity or offence, or dissatisfied with the ecclesiastical verdict, in the open court at Dunstable, called De Brois a murderer. De Brois broke out into angry and contumelious language against the judge. The insult to the justiciary was held to be insult to the king, who sought justice, where alone he could obtain it, in the bishop's court. Philip de Brois this time incurred a sentence, to our notions almost as disproportionate as that for his former offence. He was condemned to be publicly whipped, and degraded for two years from the honors and emoluments of his canonry. But to the king the verdict appeared far too lenient; the spiritual jurisdiction was accused as shielding the criminal from his due penalty.

Character of the King.

Such were the questions on which Becket was prepared to confront and to wage war to the death with the king; and all this with a deliberate knowledge both of the power and the character of Henry, his power as undisputed sovereign of England and of continental territories more extensive and flourishing than those of the king of France. These dominions included those of the Conqueror and his descendants, of the Counts of Anjou, and the great inheritance of his wife, Queen Eleanor, the old kingdom of Aquitaine; they reached from the borders of Flanders round to the foot of the Pyrenees. This almost unrivaled power could not but have worked with the strong natural passions of Henry to form the character drawn by a churchman of great ability, who would warn Becket as to the formidable adversary whom he had undertaken to oppose,—"You have to deal with one on whose policy the most distant sovereigns of Europe, on whose power his neighbors, on whose severity his subjects look with awe; whom constant successes and prosperous fortune have rendered so sensitive, that every act of disobedience is a personal outrage; whom it is as easy to provoke as difficult to appease; who encourages no rash offence by impunity, but whose vengeance is instant and summary. He will sometimes be softened by humility and patience, but will never submit to compulsion; everything must seem to be conceded by his own free will, nothing wrested from his weakness. He is more covetous of glory than of gain, a commendable quality in a prince, if virtue and truth, not the vanity and soft flattery of courtiers, awarded that glory. He is a great, indeed the greatest of kings, for he has no superior of whom he may stand in dread, no subject who dares to resist him. His natural ferocity has been subdued by no calamity from without; all who have been involved in any contest with him, have preferred the most precarious treaty to a trial of strength with one so pre-eminent in wealth, in the number of his forces, and the greatness of his puissance."[48]

A king of this character would eagerly listen to suggestions of interested or flattering courtiers, that unless the Primate's power were limited, the authority of the king would be reduced to nothing. The succession to the throne would depend entirely on the clergy, and he himself would reign only so long as might seem good to the Archbishop. Nor were they the baser courtiers alone who feared and hated Becket. The nobles might tremble from the example of De Clare, with whose powerful house almost all the Norman baronage was allied, lest every royal grant should be called in question.[49] Even among the clergy Becket had bitter enemies; and though at first they appeared almost as jealous as the Primate for the privileges of their order, the most able soon espoused the cause of the King; those who secretly favored him were obliged to submit in silence.

Parliament of Westminster.

The King, determined to bring these great questions to issue summoned a Parliament at Westminster. He commenced the proceedings by enlarging on the abuses of the archidiaconal courts. The archdeacons kept the most watchful and inquisitorial superintendence over the laity, but every offence was easily commuted for a pecuniary fine, which fell to them. The King complained that they levied a revenue from the sins of the people equal to his own, yet that the public morals were only more deeply and irretrievably depraved. He then demanded that all clerks accused of heinous crimes should be immediately degraded and handed over to the officers of his justice, to be dealt with according to law; for their guilt, instead of deserving a lighter punishment, was doubly guilty: he demanded this in the name of equal justice and the peace of the realm. Becket insisted on delay till the next morning, in order that he might consult his suffragan bishops. This the King refused: the bishops withdrew to confer upon their answer. The bishops were disposed to yield, some doubtless impressed with the justice of the demand, some from fear of the King, some from a prudent conviction of the danger of provoking so powerful a monarch, and of involving the Church in a quarrel with Henry at the perilous time of a contest for the Papacy which distracted Europe. Becket inflexibly maintained the inviolability of the holy persons of the clergy.[50] The King then demanded whether they would observe the "customs of the realm." "Saving my order," replied the Archbishop. That order was still to be exempt from all jurisdiction but its own. So answered all the bishops except Hilary of Chichester, who made the declaration without reserve.[51] The King hastily broke up the assembly, and left London in a state of consternation, the people and the clergy agitated by conflicting anxieties. He immediately deprived Becket of the custody of the Royal Castles, which he still retained, and of the momentous charge, the education of his son. The bishops entreated Becket either to withdraw or to change the offensive word. At first he declared that if an angel from Heaven should counsel such weakness, he would hold him accursed. At length, however, he yielded, as Herbert de Bosham asserts out of love for the King,[52] by another account at the persuasion of the Pope's Almoner, said to have been bribed by English gold.[53] He went to Oxford and made the concession.

Jan. 1164.

The King, in order to ratify with the utmost solemnity the concession extorted from the bishops, and even from Becket himself, summoned a great council of the realm to Clarendon, a royal palace between three and four miles from Salisbury. |Council of Clarendon.| The two archbishops and eleven bishops, between thirty and forty of the highest nobles, with numbers of inferior barons, were present. It was the King's object to settle beyond dispute the main points in contest between the Crown and the Church; to establish thus, with the consent of the whole nation, an English Constitution in Church and State. Becket, it is said, had been assured by some about the King that a mere assent would be demanded to vague and ambiguous, and therefore on occasion disputable customs. But when these customs, which had been collected and put in writing by the King's order, appeared in the form of precise and binding laws, drawn up with legal technicality by the Chief Justiciary, he saw his error, wavered, and endeavored to recede.[54] The King broke out into one of his ungovernable fits of passion. One or two of the bishops who were out of favor with the King and two knights Templars on their knees implored Becket to abandon his dangerous, fruitless, and ill-timed resistance. The Archbishop took the oath, which had been already sworn to by all the lay barons. He was followed by the rest of the bishops, reluctantly according to one account, and compelled on one side by their dread of the lay barons, on the other by the example and authority of the Primate, according to Becket's biographers, eagerly and of their own accord.[55]

Constitutions of Clarendon.

These famous constitutions were of course feudal in their form and spirit. But they aimed at the subjection of all the great prelates of the realm to the Crown to the same extent as the great barons. The new constitution of England made the bishops' fiefs to be granted according to the royal will, and subjected the whole of the clergy equally with the laity to the common laws of the land.[56] I. On the vacancy of every archbishopric, bishopric, abbey, or priory, the revenues came into the King's hands. He was to summon those who had the right of election, which was to take place in the King's Chapel, with his consent, and the counsel of nobles chosen by the King for this office. The prelate elect was immediately to do homage to the King as his liege lord, for life, limb, and worldly honors, excepting his order. The archbishops, bishops, and all beneficiaries, held their estates on the tenure of baronies, amenable to the King's justice, and bound to sit with the other barons in all pleas of the Crown, except in capital cases. No archbishop, bishop, or any other person could quit the realm without royal permission, or without taking an oath at the King's requisition, not to do any damage either going, staying, or returning, to the King or the kingdom.

II. All clerks accused of any crime were to be summoned before the King's Courts. The King's justiciaries were to decide whether it was a case for civil or ecclesiastical jurisdiction. Those which belonged to the latter were to be removed to the Bishops' Court. If the clerk was found guilty or confessed his guilt, the Church could protect him no longer.[57]

III. All disputes concerning advowsons and presentations to benefices were to be decided in the King's Courts; and the King's consent was necessary for the appointment to any benefice within the King's domain.[58]

IV. No tenant in chief of the King, none of the officers of the King's household, could be excommunicated, nor his lands placed under interdict, until due information had been laid before the King; or, in his absence from the realm, before the great Justiciary, in order that he might determine in each case the respective rights of the civil and ecclesiastical courts.[59]

V. Appeals lay from the archdeacon to the bishop, from the bishop to the Archbishop. On failure of justice by the Archbishop, in the last resort to the King, who was to take care that justice was done in the Archbishop's Court; and no further appeal was to be made without the King's consent. This was manifestly and avowedly intended to limit appeals to Rome.

All these statutes, in number sixteen, were restrictions on the distinctive immunities of the clergy; one, and that unnoticed, was really an invasion of popular freedom; no son of a villein could be ordained without the consent of his lord.

Some of these customs were of doubtful authenticity. On the main question, the exorbitant powers of the ecclesiastical courts and the immunity of the clergy from all other jurisdiction, there was an unrepealed statute of William the Conqueror. Before the Conquest the bishop sate with the alderman in the same court. The statute of William created a separate jurisdiction of great extent in the spiritual court. This was not done to aggrandize the Church, of which in some respects the Conqueror was jealous, but to elevate the importance of the great Norman prelates whom he had thrust into the English sees. It raised another class of powerful feudatories to support the foreign throne, bound to it by common interest as well as by the attachment of race. But at this time neither party took any notice of the ancient statute. The King's advisers of course avoided the dangerous question; Becket and the Churchmen (Becket himself declared that he was unlearned in the customs), standing on the divine and indefeasible right of the clergy, could hardly rest on a recent statute granted by the royal will, and therefore liable to be annulled by the same authority. The Customs, they averred, were of themselves illegal, as clashing with higher irrepealable laws.

To these Customs Becket had now sworn without reserve. Three copies were ordered to be made—one for the Archbishop of Canterbury, one for York, one to be laid up in the royal archives. To these the King demanded the further guarantee of the seal of the different parties. The Primate, whether already repenting of his assent, or under the vague impression that this was committing himself still further (for oaths might be absolved, seals could not be torn from public documents), now obstinately refused to make any further concession. The refusal threw suspicion on the sincerity of his former act. The King, the other prelates, the nobles, all but Becket,[60] subscribed and sealed the Constitutions of Clarendon as the laws of England.

April 1.

As the Primate rode from Winchester in profound silence, meditating on the acts of the council and on his own conduct, one of his attendants, who has himself related the conversation, endeavored to raise his spirits. "It is a fit punishment," said Becket, "for one who, not trained in the school of the Saviour, but in the King's court, a man of pride and vanity, from a follower of hawks and hounds, a patron of players, has dared to assume the care of so many souls."[61] De Bosham significantly reminded his master of St. Peter, his denial of the Lord, his subsequent repentance. On his return to Canterbury Becket imposed upon himself the severest mortification, and suspended himself from his function of offering the sacrifice on the altar. He wrote almost immediately to the Pope to seek counsel and absolution from his oath. He received both. The absolution restored all his vivacity.

But the King had likewise his emissaries with the Pope at Sens. He endeavored to obtain a legatine commission over the whole realm of England for Becket's enemy, Roger Archbishop of York, and a recommendation from the Pope to Becket to observe the "customs" of the realm. Two embassies were sent by the King for this end: first the Bishops of Lisieux and Poitiers; then Geoffrey Ridel, Archdeacon of Canterbury (who afterwards appears so hostile to the Primate as to be called by him that archdevil, not archdeacon), and the subtle John of Oxford. The embarrassed Pope (throughout it must be remembered that there was a formidable Antipope), afraid at once of estranging Henry, and unwilling to abandon Becket, granted the legation to the Archbishop of York. To the Primate's great indignation, Roger had his cross borne before him in the province of Canterbury. On Becket's angry remonstrance, the Pope, while on the one hand he enjoined on Becket the greatest caution and forbearance in the inevitable contest, assured him that he would never permit the see of Canterbury to be subject to any authority but his own.[62]

Becket secretly went down to his estate at Romney, near the sea-coast, in the hope of crossing the straits, and so finding refuge and maintaining his cause by his personal presence with the Pope. Stormy weather forced him to abandon his design. He then betook himself to the King at Woodstock. He was coldly received. The King at first dissembled his knowledge of the Primate's attempt to cross the sea, a direct violation of one of the constitutions; but on his departure he asked with bitter jocularity whether Becket had sought to leave the realm because England could not contain himself and the King.[63]

The tergiversation of Becket, and his attempt thus to violate one of the Constitutions of Clarendon, to which he had sworn, showed that he was not to be bound by oaths. No treaty could be made where one party claimed the power of retracting, and might at any time be released from his covenant. In the mind of Henry, whose will had never yet met resistance, the determination was confirmed, if he could not subdue the Prelate, to crush the refractory subject. Becket's enemies possessed the King's ear. Some of those enemies no doubt hated him for his former favor with the King, some dreaded lest the severity of so inflexible a prelate should curb their license, some held property belonging to or claimed by the Church, some to flatter the King, some in honest indignation at the duplicity of Becket and in love of peace, but all concurred to inflame the resentment of Henry, and to attribute to Becket words and designs insulting to the King and disparaging to the royal authority. Becket, holding such notions as he did of Church power, would not be cautious in asserting it; and whatever he might utter in his pride would be embittered rather than softened when repeated to the King.

Since the Council of Clarendon Becket stood alone. All the higher clergy, the great prelates of the kingdom, were now either his open adversaries or were compelled to dissemble their favor towards him. Whether alienated, as some declared, by his pusillanimity at Clarendon, bribed by the gifts or overawed by the power of the King, whether conscientiously convinced that in such times of schism and division it might be fatal to the interests of the Church to advance her loftiest pretensions, all, especially the Archbishop of York, the Bishops of London, Salisbury and Chichester, were arrayed on the King's side. Becket himself attributed the chief guilt of his persecution to the bishops. "The King would have been quiet if they had not been so tamely subservient to his wishes."[64]

Parliament at Northampton. Oct. 6, 1164.

Before the close of the year Becket was cited to appear before a great council of the realm at Northampton. All England crowded to witness this final strife, it might be between the royal and the ecclesiastical power. The Primate entered Northampton with only his own retinue; the King had passed the afternoon amusing himself with hawking in the pleasant meadows around. The Archbishop, on the following morning after mass, appeared in the King's chamber with a cheerful countenance. The King gave not, according to English custom, the kiss of peace.

The citation of the Primate before the King in council at Northampton was to answer a charge of withholding justice from John the Marshall employed in the king's exchequer, who claimed the estate of Pagaham from the see of Canterbury. Twice had Becket been summoned to appear in the king's court to answer for this denial of justice: once he had refused to appear, the second time he did not appear in person. Becket in vain alleged an informality in the original proceedings of John the Marshall.[65] The court, the bishops, as well as the barons, declared him guilty of contumacy; all his goods and chattels became, according to the legal phrase, at the king's mercy.[66] The fine was assessed at 500 pounds. Becket submitted, not without bitter irony: "This, then, is one of the new customs of Clarendon." But he protested against the unheard-of audacity that the bishops should presume to sit in judgment on their spiritual parent; it was a greater crime than to uncover their father's nakedness.[67] Sarcasms and protests passed alike without notice. But the bishops, all except Foliot, consented to become sureties for this exorbitant fine. |Demands on Becket.| Demands rising one above another seemed framed for the purpose of reducing the Archbishop to the humiliating condition of a debtor to the King, entirely at his disposal. First 300 pounds were demanded as due from the castles of Eye and Berkhampstead. Becket pleaded that he had expended a much larger sum on the repairs of the castles: he found sureties likewise for this payment, the Earl of Gloucester, William of Eynsford, and another of "his men." The next day the demand was for 500 pounds lent by the King during the siege of Toulouse, Becket declared that this was a gift, not a loan;[68] but the King denying the plea, judgment was again entered against Becket. At last came the overwhelming charge, an account of all the monies received during his chancellorship from the vacant archbishopric and from other bishoprics and abbeys. The debt was calculated at the enormous sum of 44,000 marks. Becket was astounded at this unexpected claim. As chancellor, in all likelihood, he had kept no very strict account of what was expended in his own and in the royal service; and the King seemed blind to this abuse of the royal right, by which so large a sum had accumulated by keeping open those benefices which ought to have been instantly filled. Becket, recovered from his first amazement, replied that he had not been cited to answer on such charge; at another time he should be prepared to answer all just demands of the Crown. He now requested delay, in order to advise with his suffragans and the clergy. He withdrew; but from that time no single baron visited the object of the royal disfavor. Becket assembled all the poor, even the beggars, who could be found, to fill his vacant board.

Takes counsel with the bishops.

In his extreme exigency the Primate consulted separately first the bishops, then the abbots. Their advice was different according to their characters and their sentiments towards him. He had what might seem an unanswerable plea, a formal acquittance from the Chief Justiciary De Luci, the King's representative, for all obligations incurred in his civil capacity before his consecration as archbishop.[69] The King, however, it was known, declared that he had given no such authority. Becket had the further excuse that all which he now possessed was the property of the Church, and could not be made liable for responsibilities incurred in a secular capacity. The bishops, however, were either convinced of the insufficiency or the inadmissibility of that plea. Henry of Winchester recommended an endeavor to purchase the King's pardon; he offered 2000 marks as his contribution. Others urged Becket to stand on his dignity, to defy the worst, under the shelter of his priesthood; no one would venture to lay hands on a holy prelate. Foliot and his party betrayed their object.[70] They exhorted him as the only way of averting the implacable wrath of the King at once to resign his see. "Would," said Hilary of Chichester, "you were no longer archbishop, but plain Thomas. Thou knowest the King better than we do; he has declared that thou and he cannot remain together in England, he as King, thou as Primate. Who will be bound for such an amount? Throw thyself on the King's mercy, or to the eternal disgrace of the Church thou wilt be arrested and imprisoned as a debtor to the Crown." The next day was Sunday; the Archbishop did not leave his lodgings. On Monday the agitation of his spirits had brought on an attack of a disorder to which he was subject: he was permitted to repose. On the morrow he had determined on his conduct. At one time he had seriously meditated on a more humiliating course: he proposed to seek the royal presence barefooted with the cross in his hands, to throw himself at the King's feet, appealing to his old affection, and imploring him to restore peace to the Church. What had been the effect of such a step on the violent but not ungenerous heart of Henry? But Becket yielded to the haughtier counsels more congenial to his own intrepid character. He began by the significant act of celebrating, out of its due order, the service of St. Stephen, the first martyr. It contained passages of holy writ (as no doubt Henry was instantly informed) concerning "kings taking counsel against the godly." The mass concluded; in all the majesty of his holy character, in his full pontifical habits, himself bearing the archiepiscopal cross, the Primate rode to the King's residence, and dismounting entered the royal hall. |Becket in the King's hall.| The cross seemed, as it were, an uplifting of the banner of the Church, in defiance of that of the King, in the royal presence;[71] or it might be in that awful imitation of the Saviour, at which no scruple was ever made by the bolder churchmen—it was the servant of Christ who himself bore his own cross. "What means this new fashion of the Archbishop bearing his own cross?" said the Archdeacon Lisieux. "A fool," said Foliot, "he always was and always will be." They made room for him; he took his accustomed seat in the centre of the bishops. Foliot endeavored to persuade him to lay down the cross. "If the sword of the King and the cross of the Archbishop were to come in conflict, which were the more fearful weapon?" Becket held the cross firmly, which Foliot and the Bishop of Hereford strove, but in vain, to wrest from his grasp.

The bishops were summoned into the King's presence: Becket sat alone in the outer hall. The Archbishop of York, who, as Becket's partisans asserted, designedly came later that he might appear to be of the King's intimate council, swept through the hall with his cross borne before him. Like hostile spears cross confronted cross.[72]

During this interval De Bosham, the archbishop's reader, who had reminded his master that he had been standard-bearer of the King of England, and was now the standard-bearer of the King of the Angels, put this question, "If they should lay their impious hands upon thee, art thou prepared to fulminate excommunication against them?" Fitz-Stephen, who sat at his feet, said in a loud clear voice, "That be far from thee; so did not the Apostles and Martyrs of God: they prayed for their persecutors and forgave them." Some of his more attached followers burst into tears. "A little later," says the faithful Fitz-Stephen of himself, "when one of the King's ushers would not allow me to speak to the Archbishop, I made a sign to him and drew his attention to the Saviour on the cross."

Condemnation of Becket.

The bishops admitted to the King's presence announced the appeal of the Archbishop to the Pope, and his inhibition to his suffragans to sit in judgment in a secular council on their metropolitan.[73] These were again direct infringements on two of the constitutions of Clarendon, sworn to by Becket in an oath still held valid by the King and his barons. The King appealed to the council. Some seized the occasion of boldly declaring to the King that he had brought this difficulty on himself by advancing a low-born man to such favor and dignity. All agreed that Becket was guilty of perjury and treason.[74] A kind of low acclamation followed which was heard in the outer room and made Becket's followers tremble. The King sent certain counts and barons to demand of Becket whether he, a liegeman of the King, and sworn to observe the constitutions of Clarendon, had lodged this appeal and pronounced this inhibition? The Archbishop replied with quiet intrepidity. In his long speech he did not hesitate for a word; he pleaded that he had not been cited to answer these charges; he alleged again the Justiciary's acquittance; he ended by solemnly renewing his inhibition and his appeal: "My person and my Church I place under the protection of the sovereign Pontiff."

The barons of Normandy and England heard with wonder this defiance of the King. Some seemed awe-struck and were mute; the more fierce and lawless could not restrain their indignation. "The Conqueror knew best how to deal with these turbulent churchmen. He seized his own brother, Odo Bishop of Bayeux, and chastised him for his rebellion; he threw Stigand, Archbishop of Canterbury, into a fetid dungeon. The Count of Anjou, the King's father, treated still worse the bishop elect of Seez and many of his clergy: he ordered them to be shamefully mutilated and derided their sufferings."

The King summoned the bishops, on their allegiance as barons, to join in sentence against Becket. But the inhibition of their metropolitan had thrown them into embarrassment, and perhaps they felt that the offence of Becket, if not capital treason, bordered upon it. It might be a sentence of blood, in which no churchman might concur by his suffrage—they dreaded the breach of canonical obedience. They entered the hall where Becket sat alone. The gentler prelates, Robert of Lincoln and others, were moved to tears; even Henry of Winchester advised the archbishop to make an unconditional surrender of his see. The more vehement Hilary of Chichester addressed him thus: "Lord Primate, we have just cause of complaint against you. Your inhibition has placed us between the hammer and the anvil: if we disobey it, we violate our canonical obedience; if we obey, we infringe the constitutions of the realm and offend the King's majesty. Yourself were the first to subscribe the customs at Clarendon, you now compel us to break them. We appeal, by the King's grace, to our lord the Pope." Becket answered "I hear."

They returned to the King, and with difficulty obtained an exemption from concurrence in the sentence; they promised to join in a supplication to the Pope to depose Becket. The King permitted their appeal. Robert Earl of Leicester, a grave and aged nobleman, was commissioned to pronounce the sentence. Leicester had hardly begun when Becket sternly interrupted him. "Thy sentence! son and Earl, hear me first! The King was pleased to promote me against my will to the archbishopric of Canterbury.

I was then declared free from all secular obligations. Ye are my children; presume ye against law and reason to sit in judgment on your spiritual father? I am to be judged only, under God, by the Pope. To him I appeal, before him I cite you, barons and my suffragans, to appear. Under the protection of the Catholic Church and the Apostolic See I depart!"[75] He rose and walked slowly down the hall. A deep murmur ran through the crowd. Some took up straws and threw them at him. One uttered the word "Traitor!" The old chivalrous spirit woke in the soul of Becket. "Were it not for my order, you should rue that word." But by other accounts he restrained not his language to this pardonable impropriety—he met scorn with scorn. One officer of the King's household he upbraided for having had a kinsman hanged. Anselm, the King's brother, he called "bastard and catamite." The door was locked, but fortunately the key was found. He passed out into the street, where he was received by the populace, to whom he had endeared himself by his charities, his austerities, perhaps by his courageous opposition to the king and the nobles, amid loud acclamations. They pressed so closely around him for his blessing that he could scarcely guide his horse. He returned to the church of St. Andrew, placed his cross by the altar of the Virgin. "This was a fearful day," said Fitz-Stephen. "The day of judgment," he replied, "will be more fearful." After supper he sent the Bishops of Hereford, Worcester, and Rochester to the King to request permission to leave the kingdom: the King coldly deferred his answer till the morrow.

Flight of Becket. Oct. 13.

Becket and his friends no doubt thought his life in danger: he is said to have received some alarming warnings.[76] It is reported, on the other hand, that the King, apprehensive of the fierce zeal of his followers, issued a proclamation that no one should do harm to the archbishop or his people. It is more likely that the King, who must have known the peril of attempting the life of an archbishop, would have apprehended and committed him to prison. Becket expressed his intention to pass the night in the church: his bed was strewn before the altar. At midnight he rose, and with only two monks and a servant stole out of the northern gate, the only one which was not guarded. He carried with him only his archiepiscopal pall and his seal. The weather was wet and stormy, but the next morning they reached Lincoln, and lodged with a pious citizen—piety and admiration of Becket were the same thing. At Lincoln he took the disguise of a monk, dropped down the Witham to a hermitage in the fens belonging to the Cistercians of Sempringham; thence by crossroads, and chiefly by night, he found his way to Estrey, about five miles from Deal, a manor belonging to Christ Church in Canterbury. He remained there a week. On

All Souls Day he went on board a boat, just before morning, and by the evening reached the coast of Flanders. To avoid observation he landed on the open shore near Gravelines. His large, loose shoes made it difficult to wade through the sand without falling. He sat down in despair. After some delay was obtained for a prelate, accustomed to the prancing war-horse or stately cavalcade, a sorry nag without a saddle, and with a wisp of hay for a bridle. But he soon got weary and was fain to walk. He had many adventures by the way. He was once nearly betrayed by gazing with delight on a falcon upon a young squire's wrist: his fright punished him for his relapse into his secular vanities. The host of a small inn recognized him by his lofty look and the whiteness of his hands. At length he arrived at the monastery of Clair Marais, near St. Omer: he was there joined by Herbert de Bosham, who had been left behind to collect what money he could at Canterbury; he brought but 100 marks and some plate. While he was in this part of Flanders the Justiciary, Richard de Luci, passed through the town on his way to England. He tried in vain to persuade the archbishop to return with him: Becket suspected his friendly overtures, or had resolutely determined not to put himself again in the King's power.

In the first access of indignation at Becket's flight the King had sent orders for strict watch to be kept in the ports of the kingdom, especially Dover. The next measure was to pre-occupy the minds of the Count of Flanders, the King of France, and the Pope against his fugitive subject. Henry could not but foresee how formidable an ally the exile might become to his rivals and enemies, how dangerous to his extensive but ill-consolidated foreign dominions. He might know that Becket would act and be received as an independent potentate. The rank of his ambassadors implied the importance of their mission to France. They were the Archbishop of York, the Bishops of London, Exeter, Chichester, and Worcester, the Earl of Arundel, and three other distinguished nobles. The same day that Becket passed to Gravelines, they crossed from Dover to Calais.[77]

Becket in exile.

The Earl of Flanders, though with some cause of hostility to Becket, had offered him a refuge; yet perhaps was not distinctly informed or would not know that the exile was in his dominions.[78] He received the King's envoys with civility. The King of France was at Compiègne. The strongest passions in the feeble mind of Louis VII. were jealousy of Henry of England, and a servile bigotry to the Church, to which he seemed determined to compensate for the hostility and disobedience of his youth.

Against Henry, personally, there were old causes of hatred rankling in his heart, not the less deep because they could not be avowed. |From 1152 to 1164.| Henry of England was now the husband of Eleanor, who, after some years of marriage, had contemptuously divorced the King of France as a monk rather than as a husband, had thrown herself into the arms of Henry and carried with her a dowry as large as half the kingdom of France. There had since been years either of fierce war, treacherous negotiations, or jealous and armed peace, between the rival sovereigns.

Louis of France.

Louis had watched, and received regular accounts of the proceedings in England; his admiration of Becket for his lofty churchmanship and daring opposition to Henry was at its height, scarcely disguised. He had already in secret offered to receive Becket, not as a fugitive, but as the sharer in his kingdom. The ambassadors appeared before Louis and presented a letter urging the King of France not to admit within his dominions the traitor Thomas, late Archbishop of Canterbury. "Late Archbishop! and who has presumed to depose him? I am a king, like my brother of England; I should not dare to depose the meanest of my clergy. Is this the King's gratitude for the services of his Chancellor, to banish him from France, as he has done from England?"[79] Louis wrote a strong letter to the Pope, recommending to his favor the cause of Becket as his own.

Ambassadors at Sens.

The ambassadors passed onwards to Sens, where resided the Pope Alexander III., himself an exile, and opposing his spiritual power to the highest temporal authority, that of the Emperor and his subservient Antipope. Alexander was in a position of extraordinary difficulty: on the one side were gratitude to King Henry for his firm support, and the fear of estranging so powerful a sovereign, on whose unrivaled wealth he reckoned as the main strength of his cause; on the other, the dread of offending the King of France, also his faithful partisan, in whose dominions he was a refugee, and the duty, the interest, the strong inclination to maintain every privilege of the hierarchy. To Henry Alexander almost owed his pontificate. His first and most faithful adherents had been Theobald the primate, the English Church, and Henry King of England; and when the weak Louis had entered into dangerous negotiations at Lannes with the Emperor; when at Dijon he had almost placed himself in the power of Frederick, and his voluntary or enforced defection had filled Alexander with dread, the advance of Henry of England with a powerful force to the neighborhood rescued the French king from his perilous position. And now, though Victor the Antipope was dead, a successor, Guido of Crema, had been set up by the imperial party, and Frederick would lose no opportunity of gaining, if any serious quarrel should alienate him from Alexander, a monarch of such surpassing power. An envoy from England, John Cummin, was even now at the imperial court.[80]

Becket's messengers, before the reception of Henry's ambassadors by Pope Alexander, had been admitted to a private interview. The account of Becket's "fight with beasts" at Northampton, and a skillful parallel with St. Paul, had melted the heart of the Pontiff, as he no doubt thought himself suffering like persecutions, to a flood of tears. How in truth could a Pope venture to abandon such a champion of what were called the liberties of the Church? He had, in fact, throughout been in secret correspondence with Becket. Whenever letters could escape the jealous watchfulness of the King, they had passed between England and Sens.[81]

The King's ambassadors at Sens.

The ambassadors of Henry were received in state in the open consistory. Foliot of London began with his usual ability; his warmth at length betrayed him into the Scriptural citation,—"The wicked fleeth when no man pursueth." "Forbear," said the Pope. "I will forbear him," answered Foliot. "It is for thine own sake, not for his, that I bid thee forbear." The Pope's severe manner silenced the Bishop of London. Hilary, Bishop of Chichester, who had overweening confidence in his eloquence, began a long harangue; but at a fatal blunder in his Latin, the whole Italian court burst into laughter.[82] The discomfited orator tried in vain to proceed. The Archbishop of York spoke with prudent brevity. The Count of Arundel, more cautious or less learned, used his native Norman. His speech was mild, grave, and conciliatory, and therefore the most embarrassing to the Pontiff. Alexander consented to send his cardinal legates to England; but neither the arguments of Foliot, nor those of Arundel, who now rose to something like a menace of recourse to the Antipope, would induce him to invest them with full power. The Pope would entrust to none but to himself the prerogative of final judgment. Alexander mistrusted the venality of his cardinals, and Henry's subsequent dealing with some of them justified his mistrust.[83] He was himself inflexible to tempting offers. The envoys privately proposed to extend the payment of Peter's Pence to almost all classes, and to secure the tax in perpetuity to the see of Rome. The ambassadors retreated in haste; their commission had been limited to a few days. The bishops, so strong was the popular feeling in France for Becket, had entered Sens as retainers for the Earl of Arundel: they received intimation that certain lawless knights in the neighborhood had determined to waylay and plunder these enemies of the Church, and of the saintly Becket.

Becket at Sens.

Far different was the progress of the exiled primate. From St. Bertin he was escorted by the Abbot, and by the Bishop of Terouenne. He entered France; he was met, as he approached Soissons, by the King's brothers, the Archbishop of Rheims, and a long train of bishops, abbots, and dignitaries of the church; he entered Soissons at the head of three hundred horsemen. The interview of Louis with Becket raised his admiration into passion. As the envoys of Henry passed on one side of the river, they saw the pomp in which the ally of the King of France, rather than the exile from England, was approaching Sens. The cardinals, whether from prudence, jealousy, or other motives, were cool in their reception of Becket. The Pope at once granted the honor of a public audience; he placed Becket on his right hand, and would not allow him to rise to speak. Becket, after a skillful account of his hard usage, spread out the parchment which contained the Constitutions of Clarendon. They were read; the whole Consistory exclaimed against the violation of ecclesiastical privileges. On further examination the Pope acknowledged that six of them were less evil than the rest; on the remaining ten he pronounced his unqualified condemnation. He rebuked the weakness of Becket in swearing to these articles, it is said, with the severity of a father, the tenderness of a mother.[84] He consoled him with the assurance that he had atoned by his sufferings and his patience for his brief infirmity. Becket pursued his advantage. The next day, by what might seem to some trustful magnanimity, to others, a skillful mode of getting rid of certain objections which had been raised concerning his election, he tendered the resignation of his archiepiscopate to the Pope. Some of the more politic, it was said, more venal cardinals, entreated the Pontiff to put an end at once to this dangerous quarrel by accepting the surrender.[85] But the Pontiff (his own judgment being supported among others by the Cardinal Hyacinth) restored to him the archiepiscopal ring, thus ratifying his primacy. He assured Becket of his protection, and committed him to the hospitable care of the Abbot of Pontigny, a monastery about twelve leagues from Sens. "So long have you lived in ease and opulence, now learn the lessons of poverty from the poor."[86] Yet Alexander thought it prudent to inhibit any proceedings of Becket against the King till the following Easter.

Effect on King Henry.

Becket's emissaries had been present during the interview of Henry's ambassadors with the Pope. Henry, no doubt, received speedy intelligence of these proceedings with Becket. He was at Marlborough after a disastrous campaign in Wales.[87] |Wrath of Henry.| He issued immediate orders to seize the revenues of the Archbishop, and promulgated a mandate to the bishops to sequester the estates of all the clergy who had followed him to France. He forbade public prayers for the Primate. In the exasperated state, especially of the monkish mind, prayers for Becket would easily slide into anathemas against the king. The payment of Peter's Pence[88] to the Pope was suspended. All correspondence with Becket was forbidden. But the resentment of Henry was not satisfied. He passed a sentence of banishment, and ordered at once to be driven from the kingdom all the primate's kinsmen, dependents, and friends. Four hundred persons, it is said, of both sexes, of every age, even infants at the breast were included (and it was the depth of winter) in this relentless edict. Every adult was to take an oath to proceed immediately to Becket, in order that his eyes might be shocked, and his heart wrung by the miseries which he had brought on his family and his friends. This order was as inhumanly executed, as inhumanly enacted.[89] It was intrusted to Randulph de Broc, a fierce soldier, the bitterest of Becket's personal enemies. It was as impolitic as cruel. The monasteries and convents of Flanders and of France were thrown open to the exiles with generous hospitality. Throughout both these countries was spread a multitude of persons appealing to the pity, to the indignation of all orders of the people, and so deepening the universal hatred of Henry. The enemy of the Church was self-convicted of equal enmity to all Christianity of heart.

Becket at Pontigny.

In his seclusion at Pontigny Becket seemed determined to compensate by the sternest monastic discipline for that deficiency which had been alleged on his election to the archbishopric. He put on the coarse Cistercian dress. He lived on the hard and scanty Cistercian diet. Outwardly he still maintained something of his old magnificence and the splendor of his station. His establishment of horses and retainers was so costly, that his sober friend, John of Salisbury, remonstrated against the profuse expenditure. Richer viands were indeed served on a table apart, ostensibly for Becket; but while he himself was content with the pulse and gruel of the monks, those meats and game were given away to the beggars. His devotions were long and secret, broken with perpetual groans. At night he rose from the bed strewn with rich coverings, as beseeming an archbishop, and summoned his chaplain to the work of flagellation. Not satisfied with this, he tore his flesh with his nails, and lay on the cold floor, with a stone for his pillow. His health suffered; wild dreams, so reports one of his attendants, haunted his broken slumbers, of cardinals plucking out his eyes, fierce assassins cleaving his tonsured crown.[90] His studies were neither suited to calm his mind, nor to abase his hierarchical haughtiness. He devoted his time to the canon law, of which the False Decretals now formed an integral part; sacerdotal fraud justifying the loftiest sacerdotal presumption. John of Salisbury again interposed with friendly remonstrance. He urged him to withdraw from these undevotional inquiries; he recommended to him the works of a Pope of a different character, the Morals of Gregory the Great. He exhorted him to confer with holy men on books of spiritual improvement.

Negotiations with the Emperor.

King Henry in the meantime took a loftier and more menacing tone towards the Pope. "It is an unheard of thing that the court of Rome should support traitors against my sovereign authority; I have not deserved such treatment.[91] I am still more indignant that the justice is denied to me which is granted to the meanest clerk." In his wrath he made overtures to Reginald, Archbishop of Cologne, the maker, he might be called, of two Antipopes, and the minister of the Emperor, declaring that he had long sought an opportunity of falling off from Alexander, and his perfidious cardinals, who presumed to support against him the traitor Thomas, late Archbishop of Canterbury.

Diet at Wurtzburg, A. D. 1165, Whitsuntide.

The Emperor met the advances of Henry with promptitude, which showed the importance he attached to the alliance. Reginald of Cologne was sent to England to propose a double alliance with the house of Swabia, of Frederick's son, and of Henry the Lion, with the two daughters of Henry Plantagenet. The Pope trembled at this threatened union between the houses of Swabia and England. At the great diet held at Wurtzburg, Frederick, asserted the canonical election of Paschal III., the new Antipope, and declared in the face of the empire and of all Christendom, that the powerful kingdom of England had now embraced his cause, and that the King of France stood alone in his support of Alexander.[92] In his public edict he declared to all Christendom that the oath of fidelity to Paschal, of denial of all future allegiance to Alexander, administered to all the great princes and prelates of the empire, had been taken by the ambassadors of King Henry, Richard of Ilchester, and John of Oxford.[93] Nor was this all. A solemn oath of abjuration of Pope Alexander was enacted, and to some extent enforced; it was to be taken by every male under twelve years old throughout the realm.[94] The King's officers compelled this act of obedience to the King, in villages, in castles, in cities.

If the ambassadors of Henry at Wurtzburg had full powers to transfer the allegiance of the King to the Antipope; if they took the oath unconditionally, and with no reserve in case Alexander should abandon the cause of Becket; if this oath of abjuration in England was generally administered; it is clear that Henry soon changed, or wavered at least in his policy. The alliance between the two houses came to nothing. Yet even after this he addressed another letter to Reginald, Archbishop of Cologne, declaring again his long cherished determination to abandon the cause of Alexander, the supporter of his enemy, the Archbishop of Canterbury. He demanded safe-conduct for an embassy to Rome, the Archbishop of York, the Bishop of London, John of Oxford, De Luci, the Justiciary, peremptorily to require the Pope to annul all the acts of Thomas, and to command the observance of the Customs.[95] The success of Alexander in Italy, aversion in England to the abjuration of Alexander, some unaccounted jealousy with the Emperor, irresolution in Henry, which was part of his impetuous character, may have wrought this change.

The monk and severe student of Pontigny found rest neither in his austerities nor his studies.[96] The causes of this enforced repose are manifest—the negotiations between Henry and the Emperor, the uncertainty of the success of the Pope on his return to Italy. It would have been perilous policy, either for him to risk, or for the Pope not to inhibit any rash measure.

Becket cites the King.

In the second year of his seclusion, when he found that the King's heart was still hardened, the fire, not, we are assured by his followers, of resentment, but of parental love, not zeal for vengeance but for justice, burned within his soul. Henry was at this time in France. Three times the exile cited his sovereign with the tone of a superior to submit to his censure. Becket had communicated his design to his followers:—"Let us act as the Lord commanded his steward:[97] 'See, I have set thee over the nations, and over the kingdoms, to root out and to pull down, and to destroy, and to hew down, to build and to plant.'"[98] All his hearers applauded his righteous resolution. In the first message the haughty meaning was veiled in the blandest words,[99] and sent by a Cistercian of gentle demeanor, named Urban.[100] The King returned a short and bitter answer. The second time Becket wrote in severer language, but yet in the spirit, 'tis said, of compassion and leniency.[101] The King deigned no reply. His third messenger was a tattered, barefoot friar. To him Becket, it might seem, with studied insult, not only intrusted his letter to the King, but authorized the friar to speak in his name. With such a messenger the message was not likely to lose in asperity. The King returned an answer even more contemptuous than the address.[102]

Nov. 11, 1165.

But this secret arraignment of the King did not content the unquiet prelate. He could now dare more, unrestrained, unrebuked. Pope Alexander had been received at Rome with open arms: at the commencement of the present year all seemed to favor his cause. The Emperor, detained by wars in Germany, was not prepared to cross the Alps. In the free cities of Italy, the anti-imperialist feeling, and the growing republicanism, gladly entered into close confederacy with a Pope at war with the Emperor. The Pontiff (secretly it should seem, it might be in defiance or in revenge for Henry's threatened revolt and for the acts of his ambassadors at Wurtzburg[103]) ventured to grant to Becket a legatine power over the King's English dominions, except the province of York. Though it was not in the power of Becket to enter those dominions, it armed him, as it was thought, with unquestionable authority over Henry and his subjects. At all events it annulled whatever restraint the Pope, by counsel or by mandate, had placed on the proceedings of Becket.[104] The Archbishop took his determination alone.[105] As though to throw an awful mystery about his plan, he called his wise friends together, and consulted them on the propriety of resigning his see. With one voice they rejected the timid counsel. Yet though his most intimate followers were in ignorance of his designs, some intelligence of a meditated blow was betrayed to Henry. The King summoned an assembly of prelates at Chinon. The Bishops of Lisieux and Seez, whom the Archbishop of Rouen, Rotran, consented to accompany as a mediator, were dispatched to Pontigny, to anticipate by an appeal to the Pope, any sentence which might be pronounced by Becket. They did not find him there: he had already gone to Soissons, on the pretext of a pilgrimage to the shrine of St. Drausus, a saint whose intercession rendered the warrior invincible in battle. Did Becket hope thus to secure victory in the great spiritual combat? One whole night he passed before the shrine of St. Drausus: another before that of Gregory the Great, the founder of the English Church, and of the see of Canterbury; and a third before that of the Virgin, his especial patroness.

Becket at Vezelay.

From thence he proceeded to the ancient and famous monastery of Vezelay.[106] The church of Vezelay, if the dismal decorations of the architecture are (which is doubtful) of that period, might seem designated for that fearful ceremony.[107] There, on the feast of the Ascension,[108] when the church was crowded with worshipers from all quarters, he ascended the pulpit, and with the utmost solemnity, condemned and annulled the Constitutions of Clarendon, declared excommunicate all who observed or enforced their observance, all who had counseled, and all who had defended them; absolved all the bishops from the oaths which they had taken to maintain them. This sweeping anathema involved the whole kingdom. But he proceeded to excommunicate by name the most active and powerful adversaries: John of Oxford, for his dealings with the schismatic partisans of the Emperor and of the Antipope, and for his usurpation of the deanery of Salisbury; Richard of Ilchester Archdeacon of Poitiers, the colleague of John in his negotiations at Wurtzburg (thus the cause of Becket and Pope Alexander were indissolubly welded together); the great Justiciary, Richard de Luci, and John of Baliol, the authors of the Constitutions of Clarendon; Randulph de Broc, Hugo de Clare, and others, for their forcible usurpation of the estates of the see of Canterbury. He yet in his mercy spared the King (he had received intelligence that Henry was dangerously ill), and in a lower tone, his voice, as it seemed, half choked with tears, he uttered his Commination. The whole congregation, even his own intimate followers, were silent with amazement.

This sentence of excommunication Becket announced to the Pope, and to all the clergy of England. To the latter he said, "Who presumes to doubt that the priests of God are the fathers and masters of kings, princes, and all the faithful?" He commanded Gilbert, Bishop of London, and his other suffragans, to publish this edict throughout their dioceses. He did not confine himself to the bishops of England; the Norman prelates, the Archbishop of Rouen, were expressly warned to withdraw from all communion with the excommunicate.[109]

Anger of the King.

The wrath of Henry drove him almost to madness. No one dared to name Becket in his presence.[110] Soon after, on the occasion of some discussion about the King of Scotland, he burst into a fit of passion, threw away his cap, ungirt his belt, stripped off his clothes, tore the silken coverlid from his bed, and crouched down on the straw, gnawing bits of it with his teeth.[111] Proclamation was issued to guard the ports of England against the threatened interdict. Any one who should be apprehended as the bearer of such an instrument, if a regular, was to lose his feet; if a clerk, his eyes, and suffer more shameful mutilation; a layman was to be hanged; a leper to be burned. A bishop who left the kingdom, for fear of the interdict, was to carry nothing with him but his staff. All exiles were to return on pain of losing their benefices. Priests who refused to chant the service were to be mutilated, and all rebels to forfeit their lands. An oath was to be administered by the sheriffs to all adults, that they would respect no ecclesiastical censure from the Archbishop.

Becket driven from Pontigny.

A second time Henry's ungovernable passion betrayed him into a step which, instead of lowering, only placed his antagonist in a more formidable position. He determined to drive him from his retreat at Pontigny. He sent word to the general of the Cistercian order that it was at their peril, if they harbored a traitor to his throne. The Cistercians possessed many rich abbeys in England; they dared not defy at once the King's resentment and rapacity. It was intimated to the Abbot of Pontigny, that he must dismiss his guest. The Abbot courteously communicated to Becket the danger incurred by the Order. He could not but withdraw; but instead now of lurking in a remote monastery, in some degree secluded from the public gaze, he was received in the archiepiscopal city of Sens; his honorable residence was prepared in a monastery close to the city; he lived in ostentatious communication with the Archbishop William, one of his most zealous partisans.[112]

Controversy with English clergy.

But the fury of haughtiness in Becket equaled the fury of resentment in the King: yet it was not without subtlety. Just before the scene at Vezelay, it has been said, the King had sent the Archbishop of Rouen and the Bishop of Lisieux to Pontigny, to lodge his appeal to the Pope. Becket, duly informed by his emissaries at the court, had taken care to be absent. He eluded likewise the personal service of the appeal of the English clergy. An active and violent correspondence ensued. The remonstrance, purporting to be from the Primate's suffragans and the whole clergy of England, was not without dignified calmness. With covert irony, indeed, they said that they had derived great consolation from the hope that, when abroad, he would cease to rebel against the King and the peace of the realm; that he would devote his days to study and prayer, and redeem his lost time by fasting, watching, and weeping; they reproached him with the former favors of the King, with the design of estranging the King from Pope Alexander; they asserted the readiness of the King to do full justice, and concluded by lodging an appeal until the Ascension-day of the following year.[113] Foliot was no doubt the author of this remonstrance, and between the Primate and the Bishop of London broke out a fierce warfare of letters. With Foliot Becket kept no terms. "You complain that the Bishop of Salisbury has been excommunicated, without citation, without hearing, without judgment. Remember the fate of Ucalegon. He trembled when his neighbor's house was on fire." To Foliot he asserted the pre-eminence, the supremacy, the divinity of the spiritual power without reserve. "Let not your liege lord be ashamed to defer to those to whom God himself defers, and calls them 'Gods.'"[114] Foliot replied with what may be received as the manifesto of his party, and as the manifesto of a party to be received with some mistrust, yet singularly curious, as showing the tone of defence taken by the opponents of the Primate among the English clergy.[115]

The address of the English prelates to Pope Alexander was more moderate, and drawn with great ability. It asserted the justice, the obedience to the Church, the great virtue and (a bold assertion!) the conjugal fidelity of the King. The King had at once obeyed the citation of the Bishops of London and Salisbury, concerning some encroachments on the Church condemned by the Pope. The sole design of Henry had been to promote good morals, and to maintain the peace of the realm. That peace had been restored. All resentments had died away, when Becket fiercely recommenced the strife; in sad and terrible letters had threatened the King with excommunication, the realm with interdict. He had suspended the Bishop of Salisbury without trial. "This was the whole of the cruelty, perversity, malignity of the King against the Church, declaimed on and bruited abroad throughout the world."[116]

John of Oxford at Rome.

The indefatigable John of Oxford was in Rome, perhaps the bearer of this address. Becket wrote to the Pope, insisting on all the cruelties of the King; he calls him a malignant tyrant, one full of all malice. He dwelt especially on the imprisonment of one of his chaplains, for which violation of the sacred person of a clerk, the King was *ipso facto* excommunicate. "Christ was crucified anew in Becket."[117] He complained of the presumption of Foliot, who had usurped the power of primate;[118] warned the Pope against the wiles of John of Oxford; deprecated the legatine mission, of which he had already heard a rumor, of William of Pavia. And all these letters, so unsparing to the King, or copies of them, probably bought out of the Roman chancery, were regularly transmitted to the King.

John of Oxford began his mission at Rome by swearing undauntedly, that nothing had been done at Wurtzburg against the power of the Church or the interests of Pope Alexander.[119] He surrendered his deanery of Salisbury into the hands of the Pope, and received it back again.[120] John of Oxford was armed with more powerful weapons than perjury or submission, and the times now favored the use of these more irresistible arms. The Emperor Frederick was levying, if he had not already set in motion, that mighty army which swept, during the next year, through Italy, made him master of Rome, and witnessed his coronation and the enthronement of the Antipope.[121] Henry had now, notwithstanding his suspicious—more than suspicious—dealings with the Emperor, returned to his allegiance to Alexander. Vast sums of English money were from this time expended in strengthening the cause of the Pope. The Guelfic cities of Italy received them with greedy hands. By the gold of the King of England, and of the King of Sicily, the Frangipani and the family of Peter Leonis were retained in their fidelity to the Pope. Becket, on the other hand, had powerful friends in Rome, especially the Cardinal Hyacinth, to whom he writes, that Henry had boasted that in Rome everything was venal. |Dec. 1166.| It was, however, not till a second embassy arrived, consisting of John Cummin and Ralph of Tamworth, that Alexander made his great concession, the sign that he was not yet extricated from his distress. He appointed William of Pavia, and Otho, Cardinal of St. Nicholas, his legates in France, to decide the cause.[122] Meantime all Becket's acts were suspended by the papal authority. At the same time the Pope wrote to Becket, entreating him at this perilous time of the Church to make all possible concessions, and to dissemble, if necessary, for the present.[123]

If John of Oxford boasted prematurely of his triumph (on his return to England he took ostentatious possession of his deanery of Salisbury[124]), and predicted the utter ruin of Becket, his friends, especially the King of France,[125] were in utter dismay at this change in the papal policy. John, as Becket had heard (and his emissaries were everywhere), on his landing in England, had met the Bishop of Hereford (one of the wavering bishops), prepared to cross the sea in obedience to Becket's citation. To him, after some delay, John had exhibited letters of the Pope, which sent him back to his diocese. On the sight of these same letters, the Bishop of London had exclaimed in the fullness of his joy, "Then our Thomas is no longer archbishop!" "If this be true," adds Becket, "the Pope has given a death-blow to the Church."[126] To the Archbishop of Mentz, for in the empire he had his ardent admirers, he poured forth all the bitterness of his soul.[127] Of the two cardinals he writes, "The one is weak and versatile, the other treacherous and crafty." He looked to their arrival with indignant apprehension. They are open to bribes, and may be perverted to any injustice.[128]

John of Oxford had proclaimed that the cardinals, William of Pavia, and Otho, were invested in full powers to pass judgment between the King and the Primate.[129] But whether John of Oxford had mistaken or exaggerated their powers, or the Pope (no improbable case, considering the change of affairs in Italy) had thought fit afterwards to modify or retract them, they came rather as mediators than judges, with orders to reconcile the contending parties, rather than to decide on their cause. The cardinals did not arrive in France till the autumn of the year.[130] Even before their arrival, first rumors, then more certain intelligence had been propagated throughout Christendom of the terrible disaster which had befallen the Emperor. Barbarossa's career of vengeance and conquest had been cut short. |A. D. 1167. Flight of Frederick.| The Pope a prisoner, a fugitive, was unexpectedly released, restored to power, if not to the possession of Rome.[131] The climate of Rome, as usual, but in a far more fearful manner, had resented the invasion of the city by the German army. A pestilence had broken out, which in less than a month made such havoc among the soldiers, that they could scarcely find room to bury the dead. The fever seemed to choose its victims among the higher clergy, the partisans of the Antipope; of the princes and nobles, the chief victims were the younger Duke Guelf, Duke Frederick of Swabia, and some others; of the bishops, those of Prague, Ratisbon, Augsburg, Spires, Verdun, Liege, Zeitz; and the arch-rebel himself, the antipope-maker, Reginald of Cologne.[132] Throughout Europe the clergy on the side of Alexander raised a cry of awful exultation; it was God manifestly avenging himself on the enemies of the Church; the new Sennacherib (so he is called by Becket) had been smitten in his pride; and the example of this chastisement of Frederick was a command to the Church to resist to the last all rebels against her power, to put forth her spiritual arms, which God would as assuredly support by the same or more signal wonders. The defeat of Frederick was an admonition to the Pope to lay bare the sword of Peter, and smite on all sides.[133]

Becket against the legates.

There can be no doubt that Becket so interpreted what he deemed a sign from heaven. But even before the disaster was certainly known he had determined to show no submission to a judge so partial and so corrupt as William of Pavia.[134] That cardinal had urged the Pope at Sens to accept

Becket's resignation of his see. Becket would not deign to disguise his contempt. He wrote a letter so full of violence that John of Salisbury,[135] to whom it was submitted, persuaded him to destroy it. A second was little milder; at length he was persuaded to take a more moderate tone. Yet even then he speaks of the "insolence of princes lifting up their horn." To Cardinal Otho, on the other hand, his language borders on adulation.

Meeting near Gisors.

The cardinal Legates traveled in slow state. They visited first Becket at Sens, afterwards King Henry at Rouen. At length a meeting was agreed on to be held on the borders of the French and English territory, between Gisors and Trie. The proud Becket was disturbed at being hastily summoned, when he was unable to muster a sufficient retinue of horsemen to meet the Italian cardinals. The two kings were there. Of Henry's prelates the Archbishop of Rouen alone was present at the first interview. Becket was charged with urging the King of France to war against his master. |Octave of St. Martin. Nov. 23.| On the following day the King of France said in the presence of the cardinals, that this impeachment on Becket's loyalty was false. To all the persuasions, menaces, entreaties of the cardinals[136] Becket declared that he would submit, "saving the honor of God, and of the Apostolic See, the liberty of the Church, the dignity of his person, and the property of the churches. As to the Customs he declared that he would rather bow his neck to the executioner than swear to observe them. He peremptorily demanded his own restoration at once to all the honors and possessions of his see." The third question was on the appeal of the bishops. Becket inveighed with bitterness on their treachery towards him, their servility to the King. "When the shepherds fled all Egypt returned to idolatry." Becket interpreted these "shepherds" as the clergy.[137] He compares them to the slaves in the old comedy; he declared that he would submit to no judgment on that point but that of the Pope himself.

The Cardinals before the King.

The Cardinals proceeded to the King. They were received but coldly at Argences, not far from Caen, at a great meeting with the Norman and English prelates. The Bishop of London entered at length into the King's grievances and his own; Becket's debt to the King,[138] his usurpations on the see of London. At the close Henry, in tears, entreated the cardinals to rid him of the troublesome churchman. William of Pavia wept, or seemed to weep from sympathy. Otho, writes Becket's emissary, could hardly suppress his laughter. The English prelates afterwards at Le Mans solemnly renewed their appeal. Their appeal was accompanied with a letter, in which they complain that Becket would leave them exposed to the wrath of the King, from which wrath he himself had fled;[139] of false representations of the Customs, and disregard of all justice and of the sacred canons in suspending and anathematizing the clergy without hearing and without trial. William of Pavia gave notice of the appeal for the next St. Martin's Day (so a year was to elapse), with command to abstain from all excommunication and interdict of the kingdom till that day.[140] Both cardinals wrote strongly to the Pope in favor of the Bishop of London.[141]

Dec. 29.

At this suspension Becket wrote to the Pope in a tone of mingled grief and indignation.[142] He described himself as the most wretched of men; applied the prophetic description of the Saviour's unequaled sorrow to himself. He inveighed against William of Pavia:[143] he threw himself on the justice and compassion of the Pope. But this inhibition was confirmed by the Pope himself, in answer to another embassage of Henry, consisting of Clarembold, Prior elect of St. Augustine's, the Archdeacon of Salisbury, and others.[144] This important favor was obtained through the interest of Cardinal John of Naples, who expresses his hope that the insolent Archbishop must at length see that he had no resource but in submission.

May 19. Becket to the Pope.

Becket wrote again and again to the Pope, bitterly complaining that the successive ambassadors of the King, John of Oxford, John Cummin, the Prior of St. Augustine's, returned from Rome each with larger concessions.[145] The Pope acknowledged that the concessions had been extorted from him. The ambassadors of Henry had threatened to leave the Papal Court, if their demands were not complied with, in open hostility. The Pope was still an exile in Benevento,[146] and did not dare to reoccupy Rome. The Emperor, even after his discomfiture, was still formidable; he might collect another overwhelming Transalpine force. The subsidies of Henry to the Italian cities and to the Roman partisans of the Pope could not be spared. The Pontiff therefore wrote soothing letters to the King of France and to Becket. He insinuated that these concessions were but for a time. "For a time!" replied Becket in an answer full of fire and passion: "and in that time the Church of England falls utterly to ruin; the property of the Church and the poor is wrested from her. In that time prelacies and abbacies are confiscated to the King's use: in that time who will guard the flock when the wolf is in the fold? This fatal dispensation will be a precedent for all ages. But for me and my fellow exiles all authority of Rome had ceased forever in England. There had been no one who had maintained the Pope against kings and princes." His significant language involves the Pope himself in the general and unsparing charge of rapacity and venality with which he brands the court of Rome. "I shall have to give an account at the last day, where gold and silver are of no avail, nor gifts which blind the eyes even of the wise."[147] |To the Cardinals.| The same contemptuous allusions to that notorious venality transpire in a vehement letter addressed to the College of Cardinals, in which he urges that his cause is their own; that they are sanctioning a fatal and irretrievable example to temporal princes; that they are abrogating all obedience to the Church. "Your gold and silver will not deliver you in the day of the wrath of the Lord."[148] On the other hand, the King and the Queen of France wrote in a tone of indignant remonstrance that the Pope had abandoned the cause of the enemy of their enemy. More than one of the French prelates who wrote in the same strain declared that their King, in his resentment, had seriously thought of defection to the Antipope, and of a close connexion with the Imperial family.[149] Alexander determined to make another attempt at reconciliation; at least he should gain time, that precious source of hope to the embarrassed and irresolute. His mediators were the Prior of Montdieu and Bernard de Corilo, a monk of Grammont.[150] It was a fortunate time, for just at this juncture, peace and even amity seemed to be established between the Kings of France and England. Many of the great Norman and French prelates and nobles offered themselves as joint mediators with the commissioners of the Pope.

Meeting at Montmirail.

A vast assembly was convened on the day of the Epiphany in the plains near Montmirail, where in the presence of the two kings and the barons of each realm the reconciliation was to take place. Becket held a long conference with the mediators. He proposed, instead of the obnoxious phrase "saving my order," to substitute "saving the honor of God;"[151] the mediators of the treaty insisted on his throwing himself on the King's mercy absolutely and without reservation. With great reluctance Becket appeared at least to yield: his counselors acquiesced in silence. With this distinct understanding the Kings of France and England met at Montmirail, and everything seemed prepared for the final settlement of this long and obstinate quarrel. |Jan. 6, 1169.| The Kings awaited the approach of the Primate. But as he was on his way, De Bosham (who always assumes to himself the credit of suggesting Becket's most haughty proceedings) whispered in his ear (De Bosham himself asserts this) a solemn caution, lest he should act over again the fatal scene of weakness at Clarendon. Becket had not time to answer De Bosham: he advanced to the King and threw himself at his feet. Henry raised him instantly from the ground. Becket, standing upright, began to solicit the clemency of the King. He declared his readiness to submit his whole cause to the judgment of the two Kings and of the assembled prelates and nobles. After a pause he added, "Saving the honor of God."[152]

Treaty broken off.

At this unexpected breach of his agreement the mediators, even the most ardent admirers of Becket, stood aghast. Henry, thinking himself duped, as well he might, broke out into one of his ungovernable fits of anger. He reproached the Archbishop with arrogance, obstinacy, and ingratitude. He so far forgot himself as to declare that Becket had displayed all his magnificence and prodigality as chancellor only to court popularity and to supplant his king in the affections of his people. Becket listened with patience, and appealed to the King of France as witness to his loyalty. Henry fiercely interrupted him. "Mark, Sire (he addressed the King of France), the infatuation and pride of the man: he pretends to have been banished, though he fled from his see. He would persuade you that he is maintaining the cause of the Church, and suffering for the sake of justice. I have always been willing, and am still willing, to grant that he should rule his Church with the same liberty as his predecessors, men not less holy than himself." Even the King of France seemed shocked at the conduct of Becket. The prelates and nobles, having in vain labored to bend the inflexible spirit of the Primate, retired in sullen dissatisfaction. He stood alone. Even John of Poitiers, his most ardent admirer, followed him to Etampes, and entreated him to yield. "And you, too," returned Becket, "will you strangle us, and give triumph to the malignity of our enemies?"[153]

The King of England retired, followed by the Papal Legates, who, though they held letters of Commination from the Pope,[154] delayed to serve them on the King. Becket followed the King of France to Montmirail. He was received by Louis; and Becket put on so cheerful a countenance as to surprise all present. On his return to Sens, he explained to his followers that his cause was not only that of the Church, but of God.[155] He passed among the acclamations of the populace, ignorant of his duplicity. "Behold the prelate who stood up even before two kings for the honor of God."

War of France and England.

Becket may have had foresight, or even secret information of the hollowness of the peace between the two kings. Before many days, some acts of barbarous cruelty by Henry against his rebellious subjects plunged the two nations again in hostility. The King of France and his prelates, feeling how nearly they had lost their powerful ally, began to admire what they called Becket's magnanimity as loudly as they had censured his obstinacy. The King visited him at Sens: one of the Papal commissioners, the Monk of Grammont, said privately to Herbert de Bosham, that he had rather his foot had been cut off than that Becket should have listened to his advice.[156]

Excommunication.

Becket now at once drew the sword and cast away the scabbard. "Cursed is he that refraineth his sword from blood." This Becket applied to the spiritual weapon. On Ascension Day he again solemnly excommunicated Gilbert Foliot Bishop of London, Joscelin of Salisbury, the Archdeacon of Salisbury, Richard de Luci, Randulph de Broc, and many other of Henry's most faithful counselors. He announced this excommunication to the Archbishop of Rouen,[157] and reminded him that whosoever presumed to communicate with any one of these outlaws of the Church by word, in meat or drink, or even by salutation, subjected himself thereby to the same excommunication. The appeal to the Pope he treated with sovereign contempt. He sternly inhibited Roger of Worcester, who had entreated permission to communicate with his brethren.[158] "What fellowship is there between Christ and Belial?" He announced this act to the Pope, entreating, but with the tone of command, his approbation of the proceeding. An emissary of Becket had the boldness to enter St. Paul's Cathedral in London, to thrust the sentence into the hands of the officiating priest, and then to proclaim with a loud voice, "Know all men, that Gilbert Bishop of London is excommunicate by Thomas Archbishop of Canterbury and Legate of the Pope." He escaped with some difficulty from ill-usage by the people. Foliot immediately summoned his clergy; explained the illegality, injustice, nullity of an excommunication without citation, hearing, or trial, and renewed his appeal to the Pope. The Dean of St. Paul's and all the clergy, excepting the priests of certain monasteries, joined in the appeal. The Bishop of Exeter declined, nevertheless he gave to Foliot the kiss of peace.[159]

Henry's intrigues in Italy.

King Henry was not without fear at this last desperate blow. He had not a single chaplain who had not been excommunicated, or was not virtually under ban for holding intercourse with persons under excommunication.[160] He continued his active intrigues, his subsidies in Italy. He bought the support of Milan, Pavia, Cremona, Parma, Bologna. The Frangipani, the family of Leo, the people of Rome, were still kept in allegiance to the Pope chiefly by his lavish payments.[161] He made overtures to the King of Sicily, the Pope's ally, for a matrimonial alliance with his family: and finally, he urged the tempting offer to mediate a peace between the Emperor and the Pope. Reginald of Salisbury boasted that, if the Pope should die, Henry had the whole College of Cardinals in his pay, and could name his Pope.[162]

New Legatine Commission. Mar. 10, 1169.

But no longer dependent on Henry's largesses to his partisans, Alexander's affairs wore a more prosperous aspect. He began, yet cautiously, to show his real bias. He determined to appoint a new legatine commission, not now rapacious cardinals and avowed partisans of Henry. The Nuncios were Gratian, a hard and severe canon lawyer, not likely to swerve from the loftiest claims of the Decretals; and Vivian, a man of more pliant character, but as far as he was firm in any principle, disposed to high ecclesiastical views. At the same time he urged Becket to issue no sentences against the King or the King's followers; or if, as he hardly believed, he had already done so, to suspend their powers.

English prelates waver.

The terrors of the excommunication were not without their effect in England. Some of the Bishops began gradually to recede from the King's party, and to incline to that of the Primate. Hereford had already attempted to cross the sea. Henry of Winchester was in private correspondence with Becket: he had throughout secretly supplied him with money.[163] Becket skillfully labored to awaken his old spirit of opposition to the Crown. He reminded Winchester of his royal descent, that he was secure in his powerful connexions; "the impious one would not dare to strike him, for fear lest his kindred should avenge his cause."[164] Norwich, Worcester, Chester, even Chichester, more than wavered. This movement was strengthened by a false step of Foliot, which exposed all his former proceedings to the charge of irregular ambition. He began to declare publicly not only that he never swore canonical obedience to Becket, but to assert the independence of the see of London and the right of the see of London to the primacy of England. Becket speaks of this as an act of spiritual parricide: Foliot was another Absalom.[165] He appealed to the pride and the fears of the Chapter of Canterbury: he exposed, and called on them to resist, these machinations of Foliot to degrade the archiepiscopal see. At the same time he warned all persons to abstain from communion with those who were under his ban; "for he had accurate information as to all who were guilty of that offence." Even in France this proceeding strengthened the sympathy with Becket. The Archbishop of Sens, the Bishops of Troyes, Paris, Noyon, Auxerre, Boulogne, wrote to the Pope to denounce this audacious impiety of the Bishop of London.

Interview of the new Legates with the King. Aug. 23.

The first interview of the new Papal legates, Gratian and Vivian, with the King, is described with singular minuteness by a friend of Becket.[166] On the eve of St. Bartholomew's Day they arrived at Damport. On their approach, Geoffrey Ridel and Nigel Sackville stole out of the town. The King, as he came in from hunting, courteously stopped at the lodging of the Legates: as they were conversing the Prince rode up with a great blowing of horns from the chase, and presented a whole stag to the Legates. The next morning the King visited them, accompanied by the Bishops of Seez and of Rennes. Presently John of Oxford, Reginald of Salisbury, and the Archdeacon of Llandaff were admitted. The conference lasted the whole day, sometimes in amity, sometimes in strife. Just before sunset the King rushed out in wrath, swearing by the eyes of God that he would not submit to their terms. Gratian firmly replied, "Think not to threaten us; we come from a court which is accustomed to command Emperors and Kings." The King then summoned his barons to witness, together with his chaplains, what fair offers he had made. He departed somewhat pacified. The eighth day was appointed for the convention, at which the King and the Archbishop were again to meet in the presence of the Legates.

Aug. 31.

It was held at Bayeux. With the King appeared the Archbishops of Rouen and Bordeaux, the Bishop of Le Mans, and all the Norman prelates. The second day arrived one English bishop—Worcester. John of Poitiers kept prudently away. The Legates presented the Pope's preceding letters in favor of Becket. The King, after stating his grievances,[167] said, "If for this man I do anything, on account of the Pope's entreaties, he ought to be very grateful." The next day at a place called Le Bar, the King requested the Legates to absolve his chaplains without any oath: on their refusal, the King mounted his horse, and swore that he would never listen to the Pope or any one else concerning the restoration of Becket. The prelates interceded; the Legates partially gave way. The King dismounted and renewed the conference. At length he consented to the return of Becket and all the exiles. He seemed delighted at this, and treated of other affairs. He returned again to the Legates, and demanded that they, or one of them, or at least some one commissioned by them, should cross over to England to absolve all who had been excommunicated by the Primate. Gratian refused this with inflexible obstinacy. The King was again furious: "I care not an egg for you and your excommunications." He again mounted his horse, but at the earnest supplication of the prelates he returned once more. He demanded that they should write to the Pope to announce his pacific offers. The Bishops explained to the King that the Legates had at last produced a positive mandate of the Pope, enjoining their absolute obedience to his Legates. The King replied, "I know that they will lay my realm under an interdict, but cannot I, who can take the strongest castle in a day, seize any ecclesiastic who shall presume to utter such an interdict?" Some concessions allayed his wrath, and he returned to his offers of reconciliation. Geoffry Ridel and Nigel Sackville were absolved on the condition of declaring, with their hands on the Gospels, that they would obey the commands of the Legates. The King still pressing the visit of one of the Legates to England, Vivian consented to take the journey. The bishops were ordered to draw up the treaty; but the King insisted on a clause "Saving the honor of his Crown." They adjourned to a future day at Caen. The Bishop of Lisieux, adds the writer, flattered the King; the Archbishop of Rouen was for God and the Pope.

Two conferences at Caen and at Rouen were equally inconclusive; the King insisted on the words, "saving the dignity of my Crown." Becket inquired if he might add "saving the liberty of the Church."[168]

The King threw all the blame of the final rupture on the Legates, who had agreed, he said, to this clause,[169] but through Becket's influence withdrew from their word.[170] He reminded the Pope that he had in his possession letters of his Holiness exempting him and his realm from all authority of the Primate till he should be received into the royal favor.[171] "If," he adds, "the Pope refuses my demands, he must henceforth despair of my good will, and look to other quarters to protect his realm and his honor." Both parties renewed their appeals, their intrigues in Rome; Becket's complaints of Rome's venality became louder.[172]

Becket began again to fulminate his excommunications. Before his departure Gratian signified to Geoffry Ridel and Nigel Sackville that their absolution was conditional; if peace was not ratified by Michaelmas, they were still under the ban. Becket menaced some old, some new victims, the Dean of Salisbury, John Cummin, the Archdeacon of Llandaff, and others.[173] But he now took a more decisive and terrible step. |Nov. 2, 1170.| He wrote to the bishops of England,[174] commanding them to lay the whole kingdom under interdict; all divine offices were to cease except baptism, penance, and the viaticum, unless before the Feast of the Purification the King should have given full satisfaction for his contumacy to the Church. This was to be done with closed doors, the laity expelled from the ceremony, with no bell tolling, no dirge wailing; all church music was to cease. The act was specially announced to the chapters of Chichester, Lincoln, and Bath. Of the Pope he demanded that he would treat the King's ambassadors, Reginald of Salisbury and Richard Barre, one as actually excommunicate, the other as contaminated by intercourse with the excommunicate.[175]

The menace of the Interdict, with the fear that the Bishops of England, all but London and Salisbury, might be overawed into publishing it in their dioceses, threw Henry back into his usual irresolution. There were other alarming signs. Gratian had returned to Rome, accompanied by William, Archbishop of Sens, Becket's most faithful admirer. Rumors spread that William was to return invested in full legatine powers—William, not only Becket's friend, but the head of the French hierarchy. If the Interdict should be extended to his French dominions, and the Excommunication launched against his person, could he depend on the precarious fidelity of the Norman prelates? Differences had again arisen with the King of France.[176] Henry was seized with an access of devotion. |Henry at Paris.| He asked permission to offer his prayers at the shrines and at the Martyrs' Mount (Montmartre) at Paris. The pilgrimage would lead to an interview with the King of France, and offer an occasion of renewing the negotiations with Becket. |Nov. 1169.| Vivan was hastily summoned to turn back. His vanity was flattered by the hope of achieving that reconciliation which had failed with Gratian. He wrote to Becket requesting his presence. Becket, though he suspected Vivian, yet out of respect to the King of France, consented to approach as near as Château Corbeil. After the conference with the King of France, two petitions from Becket, in his usual tone of imperious humility, were presented to the King of England. The Primate condescended to entreat the favor of Henry, and the restoration of the Church of Canterbury, in as ample a form as it was held before his exile. The second was more brief, but raised a new question of compensation for loss and damage during the archbishop's absence from his see.[177] |Negotiations renewed.| Both parties mistrusted each other; each watched the other's words with captious jealousy. Vivian, weary of those verbal chicaneries of the King, declared that he had never met with so mendacious a man in his life.[178] Vivian might have remembered his own retractations, still more those of Becket on former occasions. He withdrew from the negotiation; and this conduct, with the refusal of a gift from Henry (a rare act of virtue), won him the approbation of Becket. But Becket himself was not yet without mistrust; he had doubts whether Vivian's report to the Pope would be in the same spirit. "If it be not, he deserves the doom of the traitor Judas."

Henry at length, agreed that on the question of compensation he would abide by the sentence of the court of the French King, the judgment of the Gallican Church, and of the University of Paris.[179] This made so favorable an impression that Becket could only evade it by declaring that he had rather come to an amicable agreement with the King than involve the affair in litigation.

Kiss of peace.

At length all difficulties seemed yielding away, when Becket demanded the customary kiss of peace, as the pledge of reconciliation. Henry peremptorily refused; he had sworn in his wrath never to grant this favor to Becket. He was inexorable; and without this guarantee Becket would not trust the faith of the King. He was reminded, he said, by the case of the Count of Flanders, that even the kiss of peace did not secure a revolted subject, Robert de Silian, who, even after this sign of amity, had been seized and cast into a dungeon. Henry's conduct, if not the effect of sudden passion or ungovernable aversion, is inexplicable. Why did he seek this interview, which, if he was insincere in his desire for reconciliation, could afford but short delay? and from such oaths he would hardly have refused, for any great purpose of his own, to receive absolution.[180] On the other hand, it is quite clear that Becket reckoned on the legatine power of William of Sens and the terror of the English prelates, who had refused to attend a council in London to reject the Interdict. He had now full confidence that he could exact his own terms and humble the King under his feet.[181]

King's proclamation.

But the King was resolved to wage war to the utmost. Geoffry Ridel, Archdeacon of Canterbury, was sent to England with a royal proclamation containing the following articles:—I. Whosoever shall bring into the realm any letter from the Pope or the Archbishop of Canterbury is guilty of high treason. II. Whosoever, whether bishop, clerk, or layman, shall observe the Interdict, shall be ejected from all his chattels, which are confiscate to the

Crown. III. All clerks absent from England shall return before the feast of St. Hilary, on pain of forfeiture of all their revenues. IV. No appeal is to be made to the Pope or Archbishop of Canterbury under pain of imprisonment and forfeiture of all chattels. V. All laymen from beyond seas are to be searched, and if anything be found upon them contrary to the King's honor, they are to be imprisoned; the same with those who cross to the Continent. VI. If any clerk or monk shall land in England without passport from the King, or with anything contrary to his honor, he shall be thrown into prison. VII. No clerk or monk may cross the seas without the King's passport. The same rule applied to the clergy of Wales, who were to be expelled from all schools in England. Lastly, VIII. The sheriffs were to administer an oath to all freemen throughout England, in open court, that they would obey these royal mandates, thus abjuring, it is said, all obedience to Thomas, Archbishop of Canterbury.[182] The bishops, however, declined the oath; some concealed themselves in their dioceses. Becket addressed a triumphant or gratulatory letter to his suffragans on their firmness. "We are now one, except that most hapless Judas, that rotten limb (Foliot of London), which is severed from us."[183] Another letter is addressed to the people of England, remonstrating on their impious abjuration of their pastor, and offering absolution to all who had sworn through compulsion and repented of their oath.[184] The King and the Primate thus contested the realm of England.

The Pope still dubious.

But the Pope was not yet to be inflamed by Becket's passions, nor quite disposed to depart from his temporizing policy. John of Oxford was at the court in Benevento with the Archdeacons of Rouen and Seez. From that court returned the Archdeacon of Llandaff and Robert de Barre with a commission to the Archbishop of Rouen and the Bishop of Nevers to make one more effort for the termination of the difficulties. On the one hand they were armed with powers, if the King did not accede to his own terms within forty days after his citation (he had offered a thousand marks as compensation for all losses), to pronounce an interdict against his continental dominions; on the other, Becket was exhorted to humble himself before the King; if Henry was inflexible and declined the Pope's offered absolution from his oath, to accept the kiss of peace from the King's son. The King was urged to abolish in due time the impious and obnoxious Customs. And to these prelates was likewise intrusted authority to absolve the refractory Bishops of London and Salisbury.[185] This, however, was not the only object of Henry's new embassy to the Pope. He had long determined on the coronation of his eldest son; it had been delayed for various reasons. He seized this opportunity of reviving a design which would be as well humiliating to Becket as also of great moment in case the person of the King should be struck by the thunder of excommunication. The coronation of the King of England was the undoubted prerogative of the Archbishops of Canterbury, which had never been invaded without sufficient cause, and Becket was the last man tamely to surrender so important a right of his see. John of Oxford was to exert every means (what those means were may be conjectured rather than proved) to obtain the papal permission for the Archbishop of York to officiate at that august ceremony.

The absolution of the Bishops of London and Salisbury was an astounding blow to Becket. He tried to impede it by calling in question the power of the archbishop to pronounce it without the presence of his colleague. The archbishop disregarded his remonstrance, and Becket's sentence was thus annulled by the authority of the Pope. Rumors at the same time began to spread that the Pope had granted to the Archbishop of York power to proceed to the coronation. Becket's fury burst all bounds. He wrote to the Cardinal Albert and to Gratian: "In the court of Rome, now as ever, Christ is crucified and Barabbas released. The miserable and blameless exiles are condemned, the sacrilegious, the homicides, the impenitent thieves are absolved, those whom Peter himself declares that in his own chair (the world protesting against it) he would have no power to absolve.[186] Henceforth I commit my cause to God—God alone can find a remedy. Let those appeal to Rome who triumph over the innocent and the godly, and return glorying in the ruin of the Church. For me I am ready to die." Becket's fellow exiles addressed the Cardinal Albert, denouncing in vehement language the avarice of the court of Rome, by which they were brought to support the robbers of the Church. It is no longer King Henry alone who is guilty of this six years' persecution, but the Church of Rome.[187]

The coronation of the Prince by the Archbishop of York took place in the Abbey of Westminster on the 15th of June.[188] The assent of the clergy was given with that of the laity. The Archbishop of York produced a papal brief, authorising him to perform the ceremony.[189] An inhibitory letter, if it reached England, only came into the King's hand, and was suppressed; no one, in fact (as the production of such papal letter, as well as Becket's protest to the archbishop and to the bishops collectively and severally, was by the royal proclamation high treason or at least a misdemeanor) would dare to produce them.

The estrangement seemed now complete, the reconciliation more remote than ever. The Archbishop of Rouen and the Bishop of Nevers, though urged to immediate action by Becket and even by the Pope, admitted delay after delay, first for the voyage of the King to England, and secondly for his return to Normandy. Becket seemed more and more desperate, the King more and more resolute. Even after the coronation, it should seem, Becket wrote to Roger of York,[190] to Henry of Worcester, and even to Foliot of London, to publish the Interdict in their dioceses. The latter was a virtual acknowledgment of the legality of his absolution, which in a long letter to the Bishop of Nevers he had contested:[191] but the Interdict still hung over the King and the realm; the fidelity of the clergy was precarious.

Treaty of Fretteville.

The reconciliation at last was so sudden as to take the world by surprise. The clue to this is found in Fitz-Stephen. Some one had suggested by word or by writing to the King that the Primate would be less dangerous within than without the realm.[192] The hint flashed conviction on the King's mind. The two Kings had appointed an interview at Fretteville, between Chartres and Tours. The Archbishop of Sens prevailed on Becket to be, unsummoned, in the neighborhood. Some days after the King seemed persuaded by the Archbishops of Sens and Rouen and the Bishop of Nevers to hold a conference with Becket.[193] As soon as they drew near the King rode up, uncovered his head, and saluted the Prelate with frank courtesy, and after a short conversation between the two and the Archbishop of Sens, the King withdrew apart with Becket. Their conference was so long as to try the patience of the spectators, so familiar that it might seem there had never been discord between them. Becket took a moderate tone; by his own account he laid the faults of the King entirely on his evil counselors. After a gentle admonition to the King on his sins, he urged him to make restitution to the see of Canterbury. He dwelt strongly on the late usurpation on the rights of the primacy, on the coronation of the King's son. Henry alleged the state of the kingdom and the necessity of the measure; he promised that as his son's queen, the daughter of the King of France, was also to be crowned, that ceremony should be performed by Becket, and that his son should again receive his crown from the hands of the Primate.

At the close of the interview Becket sprung from his horse and threw himself at the King's feet. The King leaped down, and holding his stirrup compelled the Primate to mount his horse again. In the most friendly terms he expressed his full reconciliation not only to Becket himself, but to the wondering and delighted multitude. There seemed an understanding on both sides to suppress all points which might lead to disagreement. The King did not dare (so Becket writes triumphantly to the Pope) to mutter one word about the Customs.[194] Becket was equally prudent, though he took care that his submission should be so vaguely worded as to be drawn into no dangerous concession on his part. |July.| He abstained, too, from all other perilous topics; he left undecided the amount of satisfaction to the church of Canterbury; and on these general terms he and the partners of his exile were formally received into the King's grace. If the King was humiliated by this quiet and sudden reconcilement with the imperious prelate, to outward appearance at least he concealed his humiliation by his noble and kingly manner. If he submitted to the spiritual reproof of the prelate, he condescended to receive into his favor his refractory subject. Each maintained prudent silence on all points in dispute. Henry received, but he also granted pardon. If his concession was really extorted by fear, not from policy, compassion for Becket's six years' exile might seem not without influence. If Henry did not allude to the Customs, he did not annul them; they were still the law of the land. The kiss of peace was eluded by a vague promise. Becket made a merit of not driving the King to perjury, but he skillfully avoided this trying test of the King's sincerity.

Becket's schemes of vengeance.

But Becket's revenge must be satisfied with other victims. If the worldly King could forget the rancor of this long animosity, it was not so easily appeased in the breast of the Christian Prelate. No doubt vengeance disguised itself to Becket's mind as the lofty and rightful assertion of spiritual authority. The opposing prelates must be at his feet, even under his feet. The first thought of his partisans was not his return to England with a generous amnesty of all wrongs, or a gentle reconciliation of the whole clergy, but the condign punishment of those who had so long been the counselors of the King, and had so recently officiated in the coronation of his son.

The court of Rome did not refuse to enter into these views, to visit the offence of those disloyal bishops who had betrayed the interests and compromised the high principles of churchmen.[195] It was presumed that the King would not risk a peace so hardly gained for his obsequious prelates. |Dated Sept. 10.| The lay adherents of the King, even the plunderers of Church property were spared, some ecclesiastics about his person, John of Oxford himself escaped censure: but Pope Alexander sent the decree of suspension against the Archbishop of York, and renewed the excommunication of London and Salisbury, with whom were joined the Archdeacon of Canterbury and the Bishop of Rochester, as guilty of special violation of their allegiance to the Archbishop of Canterbury, the Bishop of

St. Asaph, and some others. Becket himself saw the policy of altogether separating the cause of the bishops from that of the King. He requested that some expressions relating to the King's excesses, and condemnatory of the bishops for swearing to the Customs, should be suppressed; and the excommunication grounded entirely on their usurpation of the right of crowning the King.[196]

Interview at Tours.

About four months elapsed between the treaty of Fretteville and the return of Becket to England. They were occupied by these negotiations at Rome, Veroli, and Ferentino; by discussions with the King, who was attacked during this period with a dangerous illness; and by the mission of some of Becket's officers to resume the estates of the see. Becket had two personal interviews with the King: the first was at Tours, where, as he was now in the King's dominions, he endeavored to obtain the kiss of peace. The Archbishop hoped to betray Henry into this favor during the celebration of the mass, in which it might seem only a part of the service.[197] Henry was on his guard, and ordered the mass for the dead, in which the benediction is not pronounced. The King had received Becket fairly; they parted not without ill-concealed estrangement. At the second meeting the King seemed more friendly; he went so far as to say, "Why resist my wishes? I would place everything in your hands." Becket, in his own words, bethought him of the tempter, "All these things will I give unto thee, if thou wilt fall down and worship me."

The King had written to his son in England that the see of Canterbury should be restored to Becket, as it was three months before his exile. But there were two strong parties hostile to Becket: the King's officers who held in sequestration the estates of the see, and seem to have especially coveted the receipt of the Michaelmas rents; and with these some of the fierce warrior nobles, who held lands or castles which were claimed as possessions of the Church of Canterbury. Randulph De Broc, his old inveterate enemy, was determined not to surrender his castle of Saltwood. It was reported to Becket, by Becket represented to the King, that De Broc had sworn that he would have Becket's life before he had eaten a loaf of bread in England. The castle of Rochester was held on the same doubtful title by one of his enemies. The second party was that of the bishops, which was powerful, with a considerable body of the clergy and laity. They had sufficient influence to urge the King's officers to take the strongest measures, lest the Papal letters of excommunication should be introduced into the kingdom.

It is perhaps vain to conjecture, how far, if Becket had returned to England in the spirit of meekness, forgiveness, and forbearance, not wielding the thunders of excommunication, nor determined to trample on his adversaries, and to exact the utmost even of his doubtful rights, he might have resumed his see, and gradually won back the favor of the King, the respect and love of the whole hierarchy, and all the legitimate possessions of his church. But he came not in peace, nor was he received in peace.[198] |Becket prepares for his return.| It was not the Archbishop of Rouen, as he had hoped, but his old enemy John of Oxford, who was commanded by the King to accompany him, and reinstate him in his see. The King might allege that one so much in the royal confidence was the best protector of the Archbishop. The money which had been promised for his voyage was not paid; he was forced to borrow £300 of the Archbishop of Rouen. He went, as he felt, or affected to feel, with death before his eyes, yet nothing should now separate him from his long-divided flock. Before his embarkation at Whitsand in Flanders, he received intelligence that the shores were watched by his enemies, it was said with designs on his life,[199] but assuredly with the determination of making a rigid search for the letters of excommunication.[200] |Letters of excommunication sent before him.| To secure the safe carriage of one of these perilous documents, the suspension of the Archbishop of York, it was intrusted to a nun named Idonea, whom he exhorts, like another Judith, to this holy act, and promises her as her reward the remission of her sins.[201] Other contraband letters were conveyed across the Channel by unknown hands, and were delivered to the bishops before Becket's landing.

The prelates of York and London were at Canterbury when they received these Papal letters. When the fulminating instruments were read before them, in which was this passage, "we will fill your faces with ignominy," their countenances fell. They sent messengers to complain to Becket, that he came not in peace, but in fire and flame, trampling his brother bishops under his feet, and making their necks his footstool; that he had condemned them uncited, unheard, unjudged. "There is no peace," Becket sternly replied, "but to men of good will."[202] It was said that London was disposed to humble himself before Becket; but York,[203] trusting in his wealth, boasted that he had in his power the Pope, the King, and all their courts.

Lands at Sandwich. Dec. 1.

Instead of the port of Dover, where he was expected, Becket's vessel, with the archiepiscopal banner displayed, cast anchor at Sandwich. Soon after his landing, appeared in arms the Sheriff of Kent, Randulph de Broc, and others of his enemies. They searched his baggage, fiercely demanded that he should absolve the bishops, and endeavored to force the Archdeacon of Sens, a foreign ecclesiastic, to take an oath to keep the peace of the realm. John of Oxford was shocked, and repressed their violence. On his way to Canterbury the country clergy came forth with their flocks to meet him; they strewed their garments in his way, chanting, "Blessed is he that cometh in the name of the Lord." |At Canterbury.| Arrived at Canterbury, he rode at once to the church with a vast procession of clergy, amid the ringing of the bells, and the chanting of music. He took his archiepiscopal throne, and afterwards preached on the text, "Here we have no abiding city." The next morning came again the Sheriff of Kent, with Randulph de Broc, and the messengers of the bishops, demanding their absolution.[204] Becket evaded the question by asserting that the Excommunication was not pronounced by him, but by his superior the Pope; that he had no power to abrogate the sentence. This declaration was directly at issue with the bull of excommunication: if the bishops gave satisfaction to the Archbishop, he had power to act on behalf of the Pope.[205] But to the satisfaction which, according to one account, he did demand, that they should stand a public trial, in other words place themselves at his mercy, they would not, and hardly could submit. They set out immediately to the King in Normandy.

The restless Primate was determined to keep alive the popular fervor, enthusiastically, almost fanatically, on his side. |Goes to London.| On a pretext of a visit to the young King at Woodstock, to offer him the present of three beautiful horses, he set forth on a stately progress. Wherever he went he was received with acclamations and prayers for his blessings by the clergy and the people. In Rochester he was entertained by the Bishop with great ceremony. In London there was the same excitement: he was received in the palace by the Bishop of Winchester in Southwark. Even there he scattered some excommunications.[206] The Court took alarm, and sent orders to the prelate to return to his diocese. Becket obeyed, but alleged as the cause of his obedience, not the royal command, but his own desire to celebrate the festival of Christmas in his metropolitan church. The week passed in holding sittings in his court, where he acted with his usual promptitude, vigor, and resolution against the intruders into livings, and upon the encroachments on his estates; and in devotions most fervent, mortifications most austere.[207]

His rude enemies committed in the mean time all kinds of petty annoyances, which he had not the loftiness to disdain. Randulph de Broc seized a vessel laden with rich wine for his use, and imprisoned the sailors in Pevensey Castle. An order from the court compelled him to release ship and crew. They robbed the people who carried his provisions, broke into his park, hunted his deer, beat his retainers; and, at the instigation of Randulph's brother, Robert de Broc, a ruffian, a renegade monk, cut off the tail of one of his state horses.

On Christmas day Becket preached on the appropriate text, "Peace on earth, good will towards men." The sermon agreed ill with the text. He spoke of one of his predecessors, St. Alphege, who had suffered martyrdom. "There may soon be a second." He then burst out into a fierce, impetuous, terrible tone, arraigned the courtiers, and closed with a fulminating excommunication against Nigel de Sackville, who had refused to give up a benefice into which, in Becket's judgment, he had intruded, and against Randulph and Robert de Broc. The maimed horse was not forgotten. He renewed in the most vehement language the censure on the bishops, dashed the candle on the pavement in token of their utter extinction, and then proceeded to the mass at the altar.[208]

The bishops with the King.

In the mean time the excommunicated prelates had sought the King in the neighborhood of Bayeux; they implored his protection for themselves and the clergy of the realm. "If all are to be visited by spiritual censures," said the King, "who officiated at the coronation of my son, by the eyes of God, I am equally guilty." The whole conduct of Becket since his return was detailed, and no doubt deeply darkened by the hostility of his adversaries. All had been done with an insolent and seditious design of alienating the affections of the people from the King. Henry demanded counsel of the prelates; they declared themselves unable to give it. But one incautiously said, "So long as Thomas lives, you will never be at peace." The King broke out into one of his terrible constitutional fits of passion; and at length let fall the fatal words, "Have I none of my thankless and cowardly courtiers who will relieve me from the insults of one low-born and turbulent priest?"

The King's fatal words.

These words were not likely to fall unheard on the ears of fierce, and warlike men, reckless of bloodshed, possessed with a strong sense of their feudal allegiance, and eager to secure to themselves the reward of desperate service. Four knights, chamberlains of the King, Reginald Fitz-Urse, William de Tracy, Hugh de Moreville, and Reginald Brito, disappeared from the court.[209] On the morrow, when a grave council was held, some barons are said, even there, to have advised the death of Becket. Milder measures were adopted: the Earl of Mandeville was sent off with orders to arrest the Primate; and as the disappearance of these four knights could not be unmarked, to stop them in the course of any unauthorized enterprise.

But murder travels faster than justice or mercy. They were almost already on the shores of England. It is said that they met in Saltwood Castle. On the 28th of December, having, by the aid of Randulph de Broc, collected some troops in the streets of Canterbury, they took up their quarters with Clarembold, Abbot of St. Augustine's.

The assassination of Becket has something appalling, with all its terrible circumstances seen in the remote past. What was it in its own age? The most distinguished churchman in Christendom, the champion of the great sacerdotal order, almost in the hour of his triumph over the most powerful king in Europe; a man, besides the awful sanctity inherent in the person of every ecclesiastic, of most saintly holiness; soon after the most solemn festival of the Church, in his own cathedral, not only sacrilegiously, but cruelly murdered, with every mark of hatred and insult. Becket had all the dauntlessness, none of the meekness of the martyr; but while his dauntlessness would command boundless admiration, few, if any, would seek the more genuine sign of Christian martyrdom.

The knights before Becket.

The four knights do not seem to have deliberately determined on their proceedings, or to have resolved, except in extremity, on the murder. They entered, but unarmed, the outer chamber.[210] The Archbishop had just dined, and withdrawn from the hall. They were offered food, as was the usage; they declined, thirsting, says one of the biographers, for blood. The Archbishop obeyed the summons to hear a message from the King; they were admitted to his presence. As they entered, there was no salutation on either side, till the Primate having surveyed, perhaps recognized them, moved to them with cold courtesy. Fitz-Urse was the spokesman in the fierce altercation which ensued. Becket replied with haughty firmness. Fitz-Urse began by reproaching him with his ingratitude and seditious disloyalty in opposing the coronation of the King's son, and commanded him, in instant obedience to the King, to absolve the prelates. Becket protested that so far from wishing to diminish the power of the King's son, he would have given him three crowns and the most splendid realm. For the excommunicated bishops he persisted in his usual evasion that they had been suspended by the Pope, by the Pope alone could they be absolved; nor had they yet offered proper satisfaction. "It is the King's command," spake Fitz-Urse, "that you and the rest of your disloyal followers leave the kingdom."[211] "It becomes not the King to utter such command: henceforth no power on earth shall separate me from my flock." "You have presumed to excommunicate, without consulting the King, the King's servant's and officers." "Nor will I ever spare the man who violates the canons of Rome, or the rights of the Church." "From whom do you hold your archbishopric?" "My spirituals from God and the Pope, my temporals from the King." "Do you not hold all from the King?" "Render unto Cæsar the things that are Cæsar's, and unto God the things that are God's." "You speak in peril of your life!" "Come ye to murder me? I defy you, and will meet you front to front in the battle of the Lord." He added, that some among them had sworn fealty to him. At this, it is said, they grew furious, and gnashed with their teeth. The prudent John of Salisbury heard with regret this intemperate language: "Would it may end well!" Fitz-Urse shouted aloud, "In the King's name I enjoin you all, clerks and monks, to arrest this man, till the King shall have done justice on his body." They rushed out, calling for their arms.

His friends had more fear for Becket than Becket for himself. The gates were closed and barred, but presently sounds were heard of those without, striving to break in. The lawless Randulph de Broc was hewing at the door with an axe. All around Becket was the confusion of terror: he only was calm. Again spoke John of Salisbury with his cold prudence—"Thou wilt never take counsel: they seek thy life." "I am prepared to die." "We who are sinners are not so weary of life." "God's will be done." The sounds without grew wilder. All around him entreated Becket to seek sanctuary in the church. He refused, whether from religious reluctance that the holy place should be stained with his blood, or from the nobler motive of sparing his assassins this deep aggravation of their crime. They urged that the bell was already tolling for vespers. He seemed to give a reluctant consent; but he would not move without the dignity of his crosier carried before him. |Becket in the Church.| With gentle compulsion they half drew, half carried him through a private chamber, they in all the hasty agony of terror, he striving to maintain his solemn state, into the church. The din of the armed men was ringing in the cloister. The affrighted monks broke off the service; some hastened to close the doors; Becket commanded them to desist—"No one should be debarred from entering the house of God." John of Salisbury and the rest fled and hid themselves behind the altars and in other dark places. The Archbishop might have escaped into the dark and intricate crypt, or into a chapel in the roof. There remained only the Canon Robert (of Merton), Fitz-Stephen, and the faithful Edward Grim. Becket stood between the altar of St. Benedict and that of the Virgin.[212] It was thought that Becket contemplated taking his seat on his archiepiscopal throne near the high altar.

The murder.

Through the open door of the cloister came rushing in the four, fully armed, some with axes in their hands, with two or three wild followers, through the dim and bewildering twilight. The knights shouted aloud, "Where is the traitor?"—No answer came back.—"Where is the Archbishop?" "Behold me, no traitor, but a priest of God!" Another fierce and rapid altercation followed: they demanded the absolution of the bishops, his own surrender to the King's justice. They strove to seize him and to drag him forth from the church (even they had awe of the holy place), either to kill him without, or to carry him in bonds to the King. He clung to the pillar. In the struggle he grappled with De Tracy, and with desperate strength dashed him on the pavement. His passion rose; he called Fitz-Urse by a foul name, a pander. These were almost his last words (how unlike those of Stephen and the greater than Stephen!) He taunted Fitz-Urse with his fealty sworn to himself. "I owe no fealty but to my King!" returned the maddened soldier, and struck the first blow. Edward Grim interposed his arm, which was almost severed off. The sword struck Becket, but slightly, on the head. Becket received it in an attitude of prayer—"Lord, receive my spirit," with an ejaculation to the Saints of the Church. Blow followed blow (Tracy seems to have dealt the first mortal wound), till all, unless perhaps De Moreville, had wreaked their vengeance. The last, that of Richard de Brito, smote off a piece of his skull. Hugh of Horsea, their follower, a renegade priest surnamed Mauclerk, set his heel upon his neck, and crushed out the blood and brains. "Away!" said the brutal ruffian, "it is time that we were gone." They rushed out to plunder the archiepiscopal palace.

The Body.

The mangled body was left on the pavement; and when his affrighted followers ventured to approach to perform their last offices, an incident occurred which, however incongruous, is too characteristic to be suppressed. Amid their adoring awe at his courage and constancy, their profound sorrow for his loss, they broke out into a rapture of wonder and delight on discovering not merely that his whole body was swathed in the coarsest sackcloth, but that his lower garments were swarming with vermin. From that moment miracles began. Even the populace had before been divided; voices had been heard among the crowd denying him to be a martyr; he was but the victim of his own obstinacy.[213] The Archbishop of York even after this dared to preach that it was a judgment of God against Becket—that "he perished, like Pharaoh, in his pride."[214] But the torrent swept away at once all this resistance. The Government inhibited the miracles, but faith in miracles scorns obedience to human laws. The Passion of the Martyr Thomas was saddened and glorified every day with new incidents of its atrocity, of his holy firmness, of wonders wrought by his remains.

Effects of the murder.

The horror of Becket's murder ran throughout Christendom. At first, of course, it was attributed to Henry's direct orders. Universal hatred branded the King of England with a kind of outlawry, a spontaneous excommunication. William of Sens, though the attached friend of Becket, probably does not exaggerate the public sentiment when he describes this deed as surpassing the cruelty of Herod, the perfidy of Julian, the sacrilege of the traitor Judas.[215]

It were injustice to King Henry not to suppose that with the dread as to the consequences of this act must have mingled some reminiscences of the gallant friend and companion of his youth and of the faithful minister, as well as religious horror at a cruel murder, so savagely and impiously executed.[216] He shut himself for three days in his chamber, obstinately refused all food and comfort, till his attendants began to fear for his life. He issued orders for the apprehension of the murderers,[217] and dispatched envoys to the Pope to exculpate himself from all participation or cognizance of the crime. His ambassadors found the Pope at Tusculum: they were at first sternly refused an audience. The afflicted and indignant Pope was hardly prevailed on to permit the execrated name of the King of England to be uttered before him. The cardinals still friendly to the King with difficulty obtained knowledge of Alexander's determination. It was, on a fixed day, to pronounce with the utmost solemnity, excommunication against the King by name, and an interdict on all his dominions, on the Continent as well as in England. The ambassadors hardly obtained the abandonment of this fearful purpose, by swearing that the King would submit in all things to the judgment of his Holiness. With difficulty the terms of reconciliation were arranged.

Reconciliation at Avranches.

In the Cathedral of Avranches in Normandy, in the presence of the Cardinals Theodin of Porto, and Albert the Chancellor, Legates for that especial purpose, Henry swore on the Gospels that he had neither commanded nor desired the death of Becket; that it had caused him sorrow, not joy; he had not grieved so deeply for the death of his father or his mother.[218] He stipulated—I. To maintain two hundred knights at his own cost in the Holy Land. II. To abrogate the Statutes of Clarendon, and all bad customs introduced during his reign.[219] III. That he would reinvest the Church of Canterbury in all its rights and possessions, and pardon and restore to their estates all who had incurred his wrath in the cause of the Primate. IV. If the Pope should require it, he would himself make a crusade against the Saracens in Spain. |Ascension Day, May 22, 1172.| In the porch of the church he was reconciled, but with no ignominous ceremony.

Throughout the later and the darker part of Henry's reign the clergy took care to inculcate, and the people were prone enough to believe, that all his disasters and calamities, the rebellion of his wife and of his sons, were judgments of God for the persecution if not the murder of the Martyr Thomas. The strong mind of Henry himself, depressed by misfortune and by the estrangement of his children, acknowledged with superstitious awe the justice of their conclusions. Heaven, the Martyr in Heaven, must be appeased by a public humiliating penance. The deeper the degradation the more valuable the atonement. In less than three years after his death the King visited the tomb of Becket, by this time a canonized saint, renowned not only throughout England for his wonder-working powers, but to the limits of Christendom. |Penance at Canterbury. Friday, July 12, 1174.| As soon as he came near enough to see the towers of Canterbury, the King dismounted from his horse, and for three miles walked with bare and bleeding feet along the flinty road. The tomb of the Saint was then in the crypt beneath the church. The King threw himself prostrate before it. The Bishop of London (Foliot) preached; he declared to the wondering multitude that on his solemn oath the King was entirely guiltless of the murder of the Saint: but as his hasty words had been the innocent cause of the crime, he submitted in lowly obedience to the penance of the Church. The haughty monarch then prayed to be scourged by the willing monks. From the one end of the church to the other each ecclesiastic present gratified his pride, and thought that he performed his duty, by giving a few stripes.[220] The King passed calmly through this rude discipline, and then spent a night and a day in prayers and tears, imploring the intercession in Heaven of him whom, he thought not now on how just grounds, he had pursued with relentless animosity on earth.[221]

Thus Becket obtained by his death that triumph for which he would perhaps have struggled in vain through a long life. He was now a Saint, and for some centuries the most popular Saint in England: among the people, from a generous indignation at his barbarous murder, from the fame of his austerities and his charities, no doubt from admiration of his bold resistance to the kingly power; among the clergy as the champion, the martyr of their order. Even if the clergy had had no interest in the miracles at the tomb of Becket, the high-strung faith of the people would have wrought them almost without suggestion or assistance. Cures would have been made or imagined; the latent powers of diseased or paralyzed bodies would have been quickened into action. Belief, and the fear of disbelieving, would have multiplied one extraordinary event into a hundred; fraud would be outbid by zeal; the invention of the crafty, even if what may seem invention was not more often ignorance and credulity, would be outrun by the demands of superstition. There is no calculating the extent and effects of these epidemic outbursts of passionate religion.[222]

Becket martyr of the clergy.

Becket was indeed the martyr of the clergy, not of the Church; of sacerdotal power, not of Christianity; of a caste, not of mankind.[223] From beginning to end it was a strife for the authority, the immunities, the possessions of the clergy.[224] The liberty of the Church was the exemption of the clergy from law; the vindication of their separate, exclusive, distinctive existence from the rest of mankind. It was a sacrifice to the deified self; not the individual self, but self as the centre and representative of a great corporation. Here and there in the long full correspondence there is some slight allusion to the miseries of the people in being deprived of the services of the exiled bishops and clergy:[225] "there is no one to ordain clergy, to consecrate virgins:" the confiscated property is said to be a robbery of the poor: yet in general the sole object in dispute was the absolute immunity of the clergy from civil jurisdiction,[226] the right of appeal from the temporal sovereign to Rome, and the asserted superiority of the spiritual rulers in every respect over the temporal power. There might, indeed, be latent advantages to mankind, social, moral, and religious, in this secluded sanctity of one class of men; it might be well that there should be a barrier against the fierce and ruffian violence of kings and barons; that somewhere freedom should find a voice, and some protest be made against the despotism of arms, especially in a newly-conquered country like England, where the kingly and aristocratic power was still foreign: above all, that there should be a caste, not an hereditary one, into which ability might force its way up, from the most low-born, even from the servile rank; but the liberties of the Church, as they were called, were but the establishment of one tyranny—a milder, perhaps, but not less rapacious tyranny—instead of another; a tyranny which aspired to uncontrolled, irresponsible rule, nor was above the inevitable evil produced on rulers as well as on subjects, from the consciousness of arbitrary and autocratic power.

Verdict of posterity.

Reflective posterity may perhaps consider as not the least remarkable point in this lofty and tragic strife that it was but a strife for power. Henry II. was a sovereign who, with many noble and kingly qualities, lived, more than even most monarchs of his age, in direct violation of every Christian precept of justice, humanity, conjugal fidelity. He was lustful, cruel, treacherous, arbitrary. But throughout this contest there is no remonstrance whatever from Primate or Pope against his disobedience to the laws of God, only to those of the Church. Becket *might*, indeed, if he had retained his full and acknowledged religious power, have rebuked the vices, protected the subjects, interceded for the victims of the King's unbridled passions. It must be acknowledged by all that he did not take the wisest course to secure this which might have been beneficent influence. But as to what appears, if the King would have consented to allow the churchmen to despise all law—if he had not insisted on hanging priests guilty of homicide as freely as laymen—he might have gone on unreproved in his career of ambition; he might unrebuked have seduced or ravished the wives and daughters of his nobles; extorted, without remonstrance of the Clergy any revenue from his subjects, if he had kept his hands from the treasures of the Church. Henry's real tyranny was not (would it in any case have been?) the object of the churchman's censure, oppugnancy, or resistance. The cruel and ambitious and rapacious King would doubtless have lived unexcommunicated and died with plenary absolution.

FOOTNOTES

[1] The "History of Latin Christianity," is now completed in six volumes.—ED.

[2] There are no less than seven full contemporary, or nearly contemporary, Lives of Becket, besides fragments, legends, and "Passions." Dr. Giles has reprinted, and in some respects enlarged, those works from the authority of MSS. I give them in the order of his volumes. I. Vita Sancti Thomæ. Auctore Edward Grim. II. Auctore Roger de Pontiniaco. III. Auctore Willelmo Filio Stephani. IV. Auctoribus Joanne Decano Salisburiensi, et Alano Abbate Teuksburiensi. V. Auctore Willelmo Canterburiensi. VI. Auctore Anonymo Lambethiensi. VII. Auctore Herberto de Bosham. Of these, Grim, Fitz-Stephen, and Herbert de Bosham were throughout his life in more or less close attendance on Becket. The learned John of Salisbury was his bosom friend and counsellor. Roger of Pontigny was his intimate associate and friend in that monastery. William was probably prior of Canterbury at the time of Becket's death. The sixth professes also to have been witness to the death of Becket. (He is called Lambethiensis by Dr. Giles, merely because the MS. is in the Lambeth Library.) Add to these the curious French poem, written five years after the murder of Becket, by Garnier of Pont S. Maxence, partly published in the Berlin Transactions, by the learned Immanuel Bekker. All these, it must be remembered, write of the man; the later monkish writers (though near the time, Hoveden, Gervase, Diceto, Brompton) of the Saint.

[3] Brompton is not the earliest writer who recorded this tale; he took it from the Quadrilogus I., but of this the date is quite uncertain. The exact date of Brompton is unknown. See preface in Twysden. He goes down to the end of Richard II.

[4] Mons. Thierry, Hist. des Normands. Lord Lyttelton (Life of Henry II.) had before asserted the Saxon descent of Becket: perhaps he misled M. Thierry.

[5] The anonymous Lambethiensis, after stating that many Norman merchants were allured to London by the greater mercantile prosperity, proceeds: "Ex horum numero fuit Gilbertus quidam cognomento Becket, patriâ Rotomagensis .... habuit autem uxorem, nomine Roseam natione Cadomensem, genere burgensium quoque non disparem."—Apud Giles, ii. p. 73.

[6] See below.

[7] "Quod si ad generis mei radicem et progenitores meos intenderis, cives quidem fuerunt Londonienses, in medio concivium suorum habitantes sine querelâ, nec omnino infimi."—Epist. 130.

[8] Grim, p. 9. Pontiniac, p. 96.

[9] Grim, p. 8.

[10] "Eo familiarius, quod præfatus Gilbertus cum domino archipræsule de propinquitate et genere loquebatur: ut ille *ortu Normannus* et circa Thierici villam de equestri ordine natu vicinus."—Fitz-Stephen, p. 184. Thiersy or Thierchville.

[11] Roger de Pontigny, p. 100.

[12] Fitz-Stephen, p. 185.

[13] According to Fitz-Stephen, Thomas was less learned (minus literatus) than his rival, but of loftier character and morals.—P. 184.

[14] "Plurimæ ecclesiæ, præbendæ nonnullæ." Among the livings were one in Kent, and St. Mary le Strand; among the prebends, two at London and Lincoln. The archdeaconry of Canterbury was worth 100 pounds of silver a-year.

[15] Epist. 130.

[16] Lord Lyttelton gives a full account of this transaction.—Book i. p. 213.

[17] This remarkable fact in Becket's history rests on the authority of his friend, John of Salisbury: "Erat enim in suspectu adolescentia regis et juvenum et pravorum hominum, quorum conciliis agi videbatur ... insipientiam et malitiam formidabat ... cancellarium procurabat in curiâ ordinari, cujus ope et operâ novi regis ne sæviret in ecclesiam, impetum cohiberet et consilii sui temperaret malitiam."—Apud Giles, p. 321. This is repeated in almost the same words by William of Canterbury, vol. ii. p. 2. Compare what may be read almost as the dying admonitions of Theobald to the king: "Suggerunt vobis filii sæculi hujus, ut ecclesiæ minuatis auctoritatem, ut vobis regni dignitas augeatur." He had before said, "Cui deest gratia Ecclesiæ, tota creatrix Trinitas adversatur."—Apud Boquet, xvi. p. 504. Also Roger de Pontigny, p. 101.

[18] Fitz-Stephen, p. 186. Compare on the office of chancellor Lord Campbell's Life of Becket.

[19] De Bosham, p. 17.

[20] See a curious passage on the singular sensitiveness of his hearing, and even of his smell.—Roger de Pontigny, p. 96.

[21] Roger de Pontigny, p. 104. His character by John of Salisbury is remarkable: "Erat supra modum captator auræ popularis ... etsi superbus esset et vanus et interdum faciem prætendebat insipienter amantium et verba proferret, admirandus tamen et imitandus erat in corporis castitate."—P. 320. See an adventure related by William of Canterbury, p. 3.

[22] Grim, p. 12. Roger de Pontigny, p. 102. Fitz-Stephen, p. 192.

[23] Fitz-Stephen, p. 191. Fitz-Stephen is most full and particular on the chancellorship of Becket.

[24] It is not quite clear how soon after the accession of Henry the appointment of the chancellor took place. I should incline to the earlier date, A. D. 1155.

[25] Fitz-Stephen, p. 187.

[26] P. 196.

[27] Edward Grim, p. 12.

[28] John of Salisbury denies that he sanctioned the rapacity of the king, and urges that he only yielded to necessity. Yet his exile was the just punishment of his guilt. "Tamen quia eum ministrum fuisse iniquitatis non ambigo, jure optimo taliter arbitror puniendum ut eo potissimum puniatur auctore, quem in talibus Deo bonorum omnium auctori præferebat.... Sed esto; nunc pœnitentiam agit, agnoscit et confitetur culpam pro ea, et si cum Saulo quandoque ecclesiam impugnavit, nunc, cum Paulo ponere paratus est animam suam."—Bouquet, p. 518.

[29] Fitz-Stephen, p. 193.

[30] Theobald died April 18, 1161. Becket was ordained priest and consecrated on Whitsunday, 1162.

[31] Yet Theobald, according to John of Salisbury, designed Becket for his successor,—

"hunc (*i. e.* Becket Cancellarium) successurum sibi sperat et orat,

Hic est carnificum qui jus cancellat iniquum,

Quos habuit reges Anglia capta diu,

Esse putans reges, quos est perpessa, tyrannos

Plus veneratur eos, qui nocuere magis."

Entheticus, l. 1295.

Did Becket decide against the Norman laws by the Anglo-Saxon? Has any one guessed the meaning of the rest of John's verses on the Chancellor and his Court? I confess myself baffled.

[32] Roger de Pontigny, p. 100.

[33] In the memorable letter of Gilbert Foliot, Dr. Lingard observes that Mr. Berington has proved this letter to be spurious. I cannot see any force in Mr. Berington's arguments, and should certainly have paid more deference to Dr. Lingard himself if he had examined the question. It seems, moreover (if I rightly understand Dr. Giles, and I am not certain that I do), that it exists in more than one MS. of Foliot's letters. He has printed it as unquestioned; no very satisfactory proceeding in an editor. The conclusive argument for its authenticity with me is this: Who, after Becket's death and canonization, would have ventured or thought it worth while to forge such a letter? To whom was Foliot's memory so dear, or Becket's so hateful, as to reopen the whole strife about his election and his conduct? Besides, it seems clear that it is either a rejoinder to the long letter addressed by Becket to the clergy of England (Giles, iii. 170), or that letter is a rejoinder to Foliot's. Each is a violent party pamphlet against the other, and of great ability and labor.

[34] Foliot's nearest relatives, if not himself, were Scotch; one of them had forfeited his estate for fidelity to the King of Scotland.—Epis. ii. cclxxviii.

[35] Read his letters before his elevation to the see of London.

[36] See, *e.g.*, Epis. cxxxi., in which he informs Archbishop Theobald that the Earl of Hereford held intercourse with William Beauchamp, excommunicated by the Primate. "Vilescit anathematis authoritas, nisi et communicantes excommunicatis corripiat digna severitas." The Earl of Hereford must be placed under anathema.

[37] Lambeth, p. 91. The election of the Bishop of Hereford to London is confirmed by the Pope's permission to elect him (March 19) rogatu H. regis et Archep. Cantuarensis. A letter from Pope Alexander on his promotion rebukes him for *fasting too severely*.—Epist. ccclix.

[38] Foliot, in a letter to Pope Alexander, maintains the superiority of Canterbury over York.—cxlix.

[39] See on the change in his habits, Lambeth, p. 48; also the strange story, in Grim, of a monk who declared himself commissioned by a preterhuman person of terrible countenance to warn the Chancellor not to dare to appear in the choir, as he had done, in a secular dress.—p. 16.

[40] Compare the letter of the politic Arnulf, Bishop of Lisieux: "Si enim favori divino favorem præferritis humanum, poteratis non solum cum summâ tranquillitate degere, sed ipso etiam magis quam olim, Principe conregnare."—Apud Bouquet, xvi. p. 229.

[41] This strange scene is recorded by Roger de Pontigny, who received his information on all those circumstances from Becket himself, or from his followers. See also Grim, p. 22.

[42] Becket had been compelled to give up the rich archdeaconry of Canterbury, which he seemed disposed to hold with the archbishopric. Geoffrey Ridel, who became archdeacon, was afterwards one of his most active enemies.

[43] The king was willing that the clerk guilty of murder or robbery should be degraded before he was hanged, but hanged he should be. The archbishop insisted that he should be safe "a læsione membrorum." Degradation was in itself so dreadful a punishment, that to hang also for the same crime was a double penalty. "If he returned to his vomit," after degradation, "he might be hanged."—Compare Grim, p. 30.

[44] "De novo judicatur Christus ante Pilatum præsidem."—De Bosham, p. 117.

[45] De Bosham, p. 100.

[46] The fairness with which the question is stated by Herbert de Bosham, the follower, almost the worshiper of Becket, is remarkable. "Arctabatur itaque rex, arctabatur et pontifex. Rex etenim populi sui pacem, sicut archipræsul cleri sui zelans libertatem, audiens sic et videns et ad multorum relationes et querimonias accipiens, per hujuscemodi castigationes, talium clericorum immo verius caracterizatorum, dæmonum flagitia non reprimi vel potius indies per regnum deterius fieri." He proceeds to state at length the argument on both sides. Another biographer of Becket makes strong admissions of the crimes of the clergy: "Sed et ordinatorum inordinati mores, inter regem et archepiscopum auxere malitiam, qui *solito abundantius* per idem tempus apparebant publicis irretiti criminibus."—Edw. Grim. It was said that no less than 100 of the clergy were charged with homicide.

[47] This, according to Fitz-Stephen, was the first cause of quarrel with the king. p. 215.

[48] See throughout this epistle of Arnulf of Lisieux, Bouquet, p. 230. This same Arnulf was a crafty and double-dealing prelate. Grim and Roger de Pontigny say that he suggested to Henry the policy of making a party against Becket among the English bishops, while to Becket he plays the

part of confidential counsellor.—Grim, p. 29. R. P., p. 119. Will. Canterb., p. 6. Compare on Arnulf, Epist. 346, v. 11, p. 189.

[49] These are the words which Fitz-Stephen places in the mouths of the king's courtiers.

[50] Herbert de Bosham, p. 109. Fitz-Stephen, p. 209, *et seq.*

[51] "Dicens se observaturos regias consuetudines bonâ fide."

[52] Compare W. Canterb., p. 6.

[53] Grim, p. 29.

[54] Dr. Lingard supposes that Becket demanded that the customs should be reduced to writing. This seems quite contrary to his policy; and Edward Grim writes thus: "Nam domestici regis, dato consentiente consilio, securem fecerant archepiscopum, quod *nunquam scriberentur* leges, nunquam illarum fieret recordatio, si eum verbo tantum in audientiâ procerum honorâsset," &c.—P. 31.

[55] See the letter of Gilbert Foliot, of which I do not doubt the authenticity.

[56] According to the Cottonian copy, published by Lord Lyttelton, Constitutions xii. xv. iv.

[57] Constitution iii.

[58] Constitutions i. and ii.

[59] Constitution vii., somewhat limited and explained by x.

[60] Herbert de Bosham. "Caute quidam non de plano negat, sed differendum dicebat adhuc."

[61] "Superbus et vanus, de pastore avium factus sum pastor ovium; dudum fautor histrionum et eorum sectator tot animarum pastor."—De Bosham, p. 126.

[62] Read the Epistles, apud Giles, v. iv. 1, 3, Bouquet, xvi. 210, to judge of the skillful steering and difficulties of the Pope. There is a very curious letter of an emissary of Becket, describing the death of the Antipope (he died at Lucca, April 21). The canons of San Frediano, in Lucca, refused to bury him, because he was already "buried in hell." The writer announces that the Emperor also was ill, that the Empress had miscarried, and that therefore all France adhered with greater devotion to Alexander; *and the Legatine commission to the Archbishop of York had expired without hope of recovery*. The writer ventures, however, to suggest to Becket to conduct himself with modesty; to seek rather than avoid intercourse with

the king.—Apud Giles, iv. 240; Bouquet, p. 210. See also the letter of John, Bishop of Poitiers, who says of the Pope, "Gravi redimit pœnitentiâ, illam qualem qualem quam Eboracensi (fecerit), concessionem."—Bouquet, p. 214.

[63] I follow De Bosham. Fitz-Stephen says that he was repelled from the gates of the king's palace at Woodstock; and that he *afterwards* went to Romney to attempt to cross the sea.

[64] "Quievisset ille, si non acquievissent illi."—Becket, Epist. ii. p. 5. Compare the whole letter.

[65] He had been sworn not on the Gospels, but on a troplogium, a book of church music.

[66] Goods and chattels at the king's mercy were redeemable at a customary fine: this fine, according to the customs of Kent, would have been larger than according to those of London.—Fitz-Stephen.

[67] "Minus fore malum verenda patris detecta deridere, quam patris ipsius personam judicare."—De Bosham, p. 135.

[68] Fitz-Stephen states this demand at 500 marks, and a second 500 for which a bond had been given to a Jew.

[69] Neither party denied this acquittance given in the King's name by the justiciary Richard de Luci. This, it should seem, unusual precaution, or at least this precaution taken with such unusual care, seems to imply some suspicion that without it, the archbishop was liable to be called to account; an account which probably, from the splendid prodigality with which Becket had lavished the King's money and his own, it might be difficult or inconvenient to produce.

[70] In an account of this affair, written later, Becket accuses Foliot of aspiring to the primacy—"et qui adspirabant ad fastigium ecclesiæ Cantuarensis, ut vulgo dicitur et creditur, in nostram perniciem, utinam minus ambitiosè, quam avidè." This could be none but Foliot.—Epist. lxxv. p. 154.

[71] "Tanquam in prœlio Domini, signifer Domini, vexillum Domini erigens; illud etiam Domini non solum spiritualiter, sed et figuraliter implens. 'Si quis,' inquit, 'vult meus esse discipulus, abneget semet ipsum, tollat crucem suam et sequatur me.'"—De Bosham, p. 143. Compare the letter of the Bishops to the Pope.—Giles, iv. 256; Bouquet, 224.

[72] "Quasi pila minantia pilis," quotes Fitz-Stephen; "Memento," said De Bosham, "quondam te extitisse regis Anglorum signiferum

inexpugnabilem, nunc vero si signifer regis Angelorum expugnaris, turpissimum."—p. 146.

[73] "Dicebant enim episcopi, quod adhuc, ipsâ die, intra decem dies datæ sententiæ, eos ad dominum Papam appellaverat, et ne de cetero eum judicarent pro seculari querelâ, quæ de tempore ante archipræsulatum ei moveretur, auctoritate domini Papæ prohibuit."—Fitz-Stephen, p. 230.

[74] Herbert de Bosham, p. 146.

[75] De Bosham's account is, that notwithstanding the first interruption, Leicester reluctantly proceeded till he came to the word "perjured," on which Becket rose and spoke.

[76] De Bosham, p. 150.

[77] Foliot and the King's envoys crossed the same day. It is rather amusing that, though Becket crossed the same day in an open boat, and, as is incautiously betrayed by his friends, suffered much from the rough sea, the weather is described as in his case almost miraculously favorable, in the other as miraculously tempestuous. So that while Becket calmly glided over, Foliot in despair of his life threw off his cowl and cope.

[78] Compare, however, Roger of Pontigny. By his account, the Count of Flanders, a relative and partisan of Henry ("consanguineus et qui partes ejus fovebat") would have arrested him. He escaped over the border by a trick.—Roger de Pontigny, p. 148.

[79] Giles, iv. 253; Bouquet, p. 217.

[80] Epist. Nuntii; Giles, iv. 254; Bouquet, p. 217.

[81] Becket writes from England to the Pope: "Quod petimus, summo silentio petimus occultari. Nihil enim nobis tutum est, quum omnia ferè referuntur ad regem, quæ nobis in conclavi vel in aurem dicuntur." There is a significant clause at the end of this letter, which implies that the emissaries of the Church did not confine themselves to Church affairs: "De Wallensibus et Oweno, qui se principem nominat, *provideatis*, quia Dominus Rex super hoc maximè motus est et indignatus." The Welsh were in arms against the King: this borders on high treason.—Apud Giles, iii. 1. Bouquet, 221.

[82] The word "oportuebat" was too bad for monkish, or rather for Roman, ears.

[83] According to Roger of Pontigny, there were some of them "qui acceptâ a rege pecuniâ partes ejus fovebant," particularly William of Pavia.—p. 153.

[84] Herbert de Bosham.

[85] Alani Vita (p. 362); and Alan's Life rests mainly on the authority of John of Salisbury. Herbert de Bosham suppresses this.

[86] The Abbot of Pontigny was an ardent admirer of Becket. See letter of the Bishop of Poitiers, Bouquet, p. 214. Prayers were offered up throughout the struggle with Henry for Becket's success at Pontigny, Citeaux, and Clairvaux.—Giles, iv. 255.

[87] Compare Lingard. Becket on this news exclaimed, as is said, "His wise men are become fools; the Lord hath sent among them a spirit of giddiness; they have made England to reel to and fro like a drunken man."—Vol. iii. p. 227. No doubt, he would have it supposed God's vengeance for his own wrongs.

[88] There are in Foliot's letters many curious circumstances about the collection and transmission of Peter's Pence. In Alexander's present state, notwithstanding the amity of the King of France, this source of revenue was no doubt important.—Epist. 149, 172, &c. Alexander wrote from Clermont to Foliot (June 8, 1165) to collect the tax, to do all in his power for the recall of Becket: to Henry, reprobating the Constitutions; to Becket, urging prudence and circumspection. This was later. The Pope was then on his way to Italy, where he might need Henry's gold.

[89] Becket, Epist. 4, p. 7.

[90] Edw. Grim.

[91] Bouquet, xvi. 256.

[92] The letters of John of Salisbury are full of allusions to the proceedings at Wurtzburg.—Bouquet, p. 524. John of Oxford is said to have denied the oath (p. 533); also Giles, iv. 264. He is from that time branded by John of Salisbury as an arch liar.

[93] John of Oxford was rewarded for this service by the deanery of Salisbury, vacant by the promotion of the dean to the bishopric of Bayeux. Joscelin, Bishop of Salisbury, notwithstanding the papal prohibition that no election should take place in the absence of some of the canons, chose the safer course of obedience to the King's mandate. This act of Joscelin was deeply resented by Becket. John of Oxford's usurpation of the deanery was one of the causes assigned for his excommunication at Vezelay. See also, on the loyal but somewhat unscrupulous proceedings of John of Oxford, the letter (hereafter referred to) of Nicholas de Monte Rotomagensi. It describes the attempt of John of Oxford to prepossess the Empress Matilda against Becket. It likewise betrays again the double-dealing of the Bishop of Lisieux, outwardly for the King, secretly a partisan and adviser of

Becket. On the whole, it shows the moderation and good sense of the empress, who disapproved of some of the Constitutions, and especially of their being written, but speaks strongly of the abuses in the Church. Nicholas admires her skillfulness in defending her son.—Giles, iv. 187. Bouquet, 226.

[94] "Præcepit enim publicè et *compulit* per vicos, per castella, per civitates ab homine sene usque ab puerum duodenum beati Petri successorem Alexandrum abjurare." William of Canterbury alone of Becket's biographers (Giles, ii. p. 19) asserts this, but it is unanswerably confirmed by Becket's Letter 78, iii. p. 192.

[95] The letter in Giles (vi. 279) is rather perplexing. It is placed by Bouquet, agreeing with Baronius, in 1166; by Von Raumer (Geschichte der Hohenstauffen, ii. p. 192) in 1165, before the Diet of Wurtzburg. This cannot be right, as the letter implies that Alexander was in Rome, where he arrived not before Nov. 1165. The embassy, though it seems that the Emperor granted the safe-conduct, did not take place, at least as regards some of the ambassadors.

[96] "Itaque per biennium ferme stetit." So writes Roger of Pontigny. It is difficult to make out so long a time.—p. 154.

[97] Herbert de Bosham.—p. 226.

[98] Jer. i. 10.

[99] "Suavissimas literas, supplicationem solam, correptionem vero nullam vel *modicam* continentes."—De Bosham.

[100] Urbane by disposition as by name.—Ibid.

[101] Giles, iii. 365. Bouquet, p. 243.

[102] "Quin potius dura propinantes, dura pro duris, immo multo plus duriora prioribus, reportaverunt."—De Bosham.

[103] The Pope had written (Jan. 28) to the bishops of England not to presume to act without the consent of Thomas, Archbishop of Canterbury. April 5, he forbade Roger of York and the other prelates to crown the King's son. May 3, he writes to Foliot and the bishops who had received benefices of the King to surrender them under pain of anathema; to Becket in favor of Joscelin, Bishop of Salisbury: he had annulled the grant of the deanery of Salisbury to John of Oxford. May 10, to the Archbishop of Rouen, denouncing the dealings of Henry with the Emperor and the Antipope.—Giles, iv. 10 *a* 80. Bouquet, 246.

[104] The inhibition given at Sens to proceed against the King, before the Easter of the following year (A. D. 1166), had now expired. Moreover

he had a direct commission to proceed by Commination against those who forcibly withheld the property of the see of Canterbury.—Apud Giles, iv. 8. Bouquet, xvi. 844. At the same time the Pope urged great discretion as to the King's person. Giles, iv. 12. Bouquet, 244.

[105] At the same time Becket wrote to Foliot of London, commanding him under penalty of excommunication to transmit to him the sequestered revenues of Canterbury in his hands.—Foliot appealed to the Pope.—Foliot's Letter. Giles, vi. 5. Bouquet, 215.

[106] The curious History of the Monastery of Vezelay, by Hugh of Poitiers (translated in Guizot, Collection des Mémoires), though it twice mentions Becket, stops just short of this excommunication, 1166. Vezelay boasted to be subject only to the See of Rome, to have been made by its founder part of the patrimony of St. Peter. This was one great distinction: the other was the unquestioned possession of the body of St. Mary Magdalene, "l'amie de Dieu." Vezelay had been in constant strife with the Bishop of Autun for its ecclesiastical, with the Count of Nevers for its territorial, independence; with the monastery of Clugny, as its rival. This is a document very instructive as to the life of the age.

[107] A modern traveller thus writes of the church of Vezelay: "On voit par le choix des sujets qui ont un sens, quel était l'esprit du temps et la manière d'interpréter la religion. Ce n'était pas par la douceur ou la persuasion qu'on voulait convertir, mais bien par la terreur. Les discours des prêtres pourraient se résumer en ce peu de mots: 'Croyez, ou sinon vous périssez misérablement, et vous serez éternellement tourmentés dans l'autre monde!' De leur côté les artistes, gens religieux, ecclésiastiques même pour la plupart, donnaient une forme réelle aux sombres images que leur inspirait un zèle farouche. Je ne trouve à Vezelay aucun de ces sujets que les ames tendres aimeraient à retracer, tels que le pardon accordé au repentir, la récompense du juste, &c.; mais au contraire, je vois Samuel égorgeant Agag; des diables écartelant des damnés, ou les entraînant dans l'abîme; puis des animaux horribles, des monstres hideux, des têtes grimaçantes exprimant ou les souffrances des reprouvés, ou la joie des habitans de l'enfer. Qu'on se représente la dévotion des hommes élevés au milieu de ces images, et l'on s'étonnera moins des massacres des Albigeois."—Notes d'un Voyage dans le Midi de la France, par Prosper Merimée, p. 43.

[108] Diceto gives the date Ascension Day, Herbert de Bosham St. Mary Magdalene's Day (July 22d). It should seem that De Bosham's memory failed him. See the letter of Nicolas de M. Rotomagensi, who speaks of the excommunication as past, and that Becket was expected to excommunicate *the King* on St. Mary Magdalene's Day. This, if done at

Vezelay (as it were, over the body of the Saint, on her sacred day), had been tenfold more awful.

[109] See the curious letter of Nicolas de Monte Rotomagensi, Giles iv., Bouquet, 250. This measure of Becket was imputed by the Archbishop of Rheims to pride or anger ("extollentiæ aut iræ"): it made an unfavorable impression on the Empress Matilda.—Ibid.

[110] Epist. Giles, iv. 185; Bouquet, 258.

[111] Epist. Giles, iv. 260; Bouquet, 256.

[112] Herbert de Bosham, p. 232.

[113] Epist. Giles, vi. 158; Bouquet, 259.

[114] "Non indignetur itaque Dominus noster deferre illis, quibus summus omnium deferre non dedignatur, Deos appellans eos sæpius in sacris literis. Sic enim dixit, 'Ego dixit, Dii estis,' et 'Constituti te Deum Pharaonis,' et 'Deis non detrahere.'"—Epist. Giles, iii. p. 287; Bouquet, 261.

[115] Foliot took the precaution of paying into the exchequer all that he had received from the sequestered property of the see of Canterbury.—Giles, v. p. 265. Lyttelton in Appendice.

[116] "Hæc est Domini regis toto orbe declamata crudelitas, hæc ab eo persecutio, hæc operum ejus perversorum rumusculis undique divulgata malignitas."—Giles, vi. 190; Bouquet, 265.

[117] Giles, iii. 6; Bouquet, 266. Compare letter of Bishop Elect of Chartres.—Giles, vi. 211; Bouquet, 269.

[118] Foliot obtained letters either at this time or somewhat later from his own Chapter of St. Paul, from many of the greatest dignitaries of the English Church, the abbots of Westminster and Reading, and from some distinguished foreign ecclesiastics, in favor of himself, his piety, churchmanship, and impartiality.

[119] The German accounts are unanimous about the proceedings at Wurtzburg and the oath of the English ambassadors. See the account in Von Raumer (*loc. cit.*), especially of the conduct of Reginald of Cologne, and the authorities. John of Oxford is henceforth called, in John of Salisbury's letters, jurator. Becket repeatedly charges him with perjury.—Giles, iii. p. 129 and 351; Bouquet, 280. Becket there says that John of Oxford had given up part of the "customs." He begs John of Poitiers to let the King know this. See the very curious answer of John of Poitiers.—Giles, vi. 251; Bouquet, 280. It appears that as all Becket's letters to the Pope were copied and transmitted from Rome to Henry, so John of

Poitiers, outwardly the King's loyal subject, is the secret spy of Becket. He speaks of those in England who thirst after Becket's blood.

[120] The Pope acknowledges that this was extorted from him by fear of Henry, and makes an awkward apology to Becket.—Giles, iv. 18; Bouquet, 309.

[121] He was crowned in Rome August 1. Compare next chapter—Sismondi, Républiques Italiennes, ii. ch. x.; Von Raumer, ii. p. 209, &c.

[122] Giles, iii. 128; Bouquet, 272. Compare Letters to Cardinals Boso and Henry.—Giles, iii. 103, 113; Bouquet, 174. Letter to Henry announcing the appointment, December 20.

[123] "Si non omnia secundum beneplacitum succedant, ad præsens dissimulet."—Giles, vi. 15; Bouquet, 277.

[124] See the curious letter of Master Lombard, Becket's instructor in the canon law, who boldly remonstrates with the Pope. He asserts that Henry was so frightened at the menace of excommunication, his subjects, even the bishops, at that of his interdict, that they were in despair. Their only hope was in the death or some great disaster of the Pope.—Giles, iv. 208; Bouquet, 282.

[125] See Letters of Louis; Giles, iv. 308; Bouquet, 287.

[126] "Strangulavit," a favorite word.—Giles, iii. 214; Bouquet, 284.

[127] Giles, iii. 235; Bouquet, 285.

[128] Compare John of Salisbury, p. 539. "Scripsit autem rex Domino *Coloniensis*, Henricum Pisanum et Willelmum Papiensem in Franciam venturos ad novas exactiones faciendas, ut undique conradant et contrahant, unde Papa Alexander in urbe sustentetur; alter, ut nostis, levis est et mutabilis, alter dolosus et fraudulentus, uterque cupidus et avarus: et ideo de facili munera cœnabunt eos et ad omnem injustitiam incurvabunt. Audito eorum detestando adventu formidare cæpi præsentiam eorum causæ vestræ multum nocituram; et ne vestro et vestrorum sanguine gratiam Regis Angliæ redimere non erubescant." He refers with great joy to the insurrection of the Saxons against the Emperor. He says elsewhere of Henry of Pisa, "Vir bonæ opinionis est, sed Romanus et Cardinalis."—Epist. cc. ii.

[129] The English bishops declare to the Pope himself that they had received this concession, *scripto formatum*, from the Pope, and that the King was furious at what he thought a deception.—Giles, vi. 194; Bouquet, 304.

[130] The Pope wrote to the legates to soothe Becket and the King of France; he accuses John of Oxford of spreading false reports about the

extent of their commission; John Cummin of betraying his letters to the Antipope.—Giles, vi. 54.

[131] So completely does Becket's fortune follow that of the Pope, that on June 17 Alexander writes to permit Roger of York to crown the King's son; no sooner is he safe in Benevento, August 22 (perhaps the fever had begun), than he writes to his legates to confirm the excommunications of Becket, which he had suspended.

[132] Muratori, sub ann. 1167; Von Raumer, ii. 210. On the 1st of August Frederick was crowned; September 4, he is at the Pass of Pontremoli, in full retreat, or rather flight.

[133] In a curious passage in a letter written by Herbert de Bosham in the name of Becket, Frederick's defeat is compared to Henry's disgraceful campaign in Wales. "My enemy," says Becket, "in the abundance of his valor, could not prevail against a breechless and ragged people ('exbraccatum et pannosum')."—Giles, viii. p. 268.

[134] "Credimus non esse juri consentaneum, nos ejus subire judicium vel examen qui quærit sibi facere commercium de sanguine nostro, de pretio utinam non iniquitatis, quærit sibi nomen et gloriam."—D. Thom. Epist. Giles, iii. p. 15. The two legates are described as "plus avaritiæ quam justitiæ studiosi."—W. Cant. p. 21.

[135] Giles, iii. 157, and John of Salisbury's remarkable expostulatory letter upon Becket's violence.—Bouquet, p. 566.

[136] Herbert de Bosham, p. 248; Epist. Giles, iii. 16; Bouquet, 296.

[137] Giles, iii. p. 21. Compare the whole letter.

[138] Foliot rather profanely said, the primate seems to think that as sin is washed away in baptism, so debts are cancelled by promotion.

[139] "Ad mortem nos invitat et sanguinis effusionem, cum ipse mortem, quam nemo sibi dignabatur aut minabatur inferre, summo studio declinaverit et suum sanguinem illibatum conservando, ejus nec guttam effundi voluerit."—Giles vi. 196. Bouquet, 304.

[140] Giles, vi. 148. Bouquet, 304.

[141] Giles, vi. 135, 141. Bouquet, 306. William of Pavia recommended the translation of Becket to some other see.

[142] Giles, iii. 28. Bouquet, 306.

[143] One of his letters to William of Pavia begins with this fierce denunciation: "Non credebam me tibi venalem proponendum emptoribus, ut de sanguine meo compareres tibi compendium de pretio iniquitatis,

faciens tibi nomen et gloriam."—Giles, iii. 153. Becket always represents his enemies as thirsting after his blood.

[144] Giles, iv. 128; vi. 133. Bouquet, 312, 313.

[145] Epist. Giles, ii. 24.

[146] He was at Benevento, though with different degrees of power, from August 22, 1167, to Feb. 24, 1170.

[147] Giles, iii. p. 55. Bouquet, 317. Read the whole letter beginning "Anima mea."

[148] Bouquet, 324.

[149] Epist. Giles, iv. Bouquet, 320.

[150] Their instructions are dated May 25, 1168. See also the wavering letters to Becket and the King of France.—Giles, iv. p. 25, p. 111.

[151] "Sed quid? Nobis ita consilium suspendentibus et hæsitantibus quid agendum a pacis mediatoribus, multis et magnis viris, et præsertim qui inter ipsos a viris religiosis et aliis archipræsuli amicissimis et familiarissimis, adeo sicut et supra diximus, suasus, tractus et impulsus est, ut haberetur persuasus."—De Bosham, p. 268.

[152] "Sed mox adjecit, quod nec rex nec pacis mediatores, vel alii, vel etiam sui propriè æstimaverunt, ut adjiceret videlicet 'Salvo honore Dei.'"—De Bosham, p. 262. In his account to the Pope of this meeting, Becket suppresses his own tergiversation on this point.—Epist. Giles, iii. p. 43. Compare John of Salisbury (who was not present). Bouquet, 395.

[153] "Ut quid nos et vos strangulatis?"—Epist. Giles, iii. 312.

[154] Throughout the Pope kept up his false game. He privately assured the King of France that he need not be alarmed if himself (Alexander) seemed to take part against the archbishop. The cause was safe in his bosom. See the curious letter of Matthew of Sens.—Epist. Giles, iv. p. 166.

[155] "Nunc præter ecclesiæ causam, expressam ipsius etiam Dei causam agebamus."—De Bosham, 272.

[156] De Bosham, 278.

[157] Giles, iii. 290; vi. 293. Bouquet, 346.

[158] Giles, iii. 322. Bouquet, 348.

[159] Epist. Giles, iv. 225.

[160] Fragm. Vit. Giles, i. p. 371.

[161] "Et quod omnes Romanos datâ pecuniâ inducant ut faciant fidelitatem domino Papæ, dummodo in nostrâ dejectione regis Angliæ satisfaciat voluntati."—Epist. ad Humbold. Card. Giles, iii. 123. Bouquet, 350. Compare Lambeth, on the effect of Italian affairs on the conduct of the Pope.—p. 106.

[162] Epist. 188, p. 266.

[163] Fitz-Stephen, p. 271.

[164] "Domo vestra flagellum suspendit impius, ne quod promereret, propinquorum vestrorum ministerio veniat super eum."—Giles, iii. 338. Bouquet, 358.

[165] Giles, iii. 201. Bouquet, 361.

[166] "Amici ad Thomam."—Giles, iv. 277. Bouquet, 370.

[167] Henry, it should be observed, waived all the demands which he had hitherto urged against Becket, for debts incurred during his chancellorship.

[168] Epist. Giles, iv. 216. Bouquet, 373.

[169] "Revocato consensu," writes the Bishop of Nevers, a moderate prelate, who regrets the obstinacy of the nuncios. Giles, vi. 266. Bouquet, 377. Compare the letter of the clergy of Normandy to the Pope.—Giles, vi. 177. Bouquet, 377.

[170] Becket thought, or pretended to think, that under the "dignitatibus" lurked the "consuetudinibus."—Giles, iii. 299. Bouquet, 379.

[171] "Ceteras vestras recepimus, et ipsas adhuc penes nos habemus, in quibus terram nostram et personas regni a præfata Cantuarensis potestate eximebatis, donec ipse in gratiam nostram rediisset."—Epist. Giles, vi. 291. Bouquet, 374.

[172] "Nam quod mundus sentit, dolet, ingemiscit, nullus adeo iniquam causam ad ecclesiam Romanam defert, quin ibi spe lucri concepta ne dixerim odore sordium, adjutorem inveniat et patronum."—Epist. iii. 133; Bouquet, 382.

[173] Giles, iii. 250; Bouquet, 387.

[174] Giles, iii. 334; Bouquet, 388.

[175] Giles, iii. 42; Bouquet, 390. Reginald of Salisbury was an especial object of Becket's hate. He calls him one born in fornication ("fornicarium"), son of a priest. Reginald hated Becket with equal cordiality. Becket had betrayed him by a false promise of not injuring his

father. "Quod utique ipsi non plus quam cani faceremus."—This letter contains Reginald's speech about Henry having the College of Cardinals in his pay.—Giles, iii. 225; Bouquet, 391.

[176] Becket writes to the Pope, January 1170. "Nec vos oportet de cætero vereri, ne transeat ad schismaticos, quod sic eum Christus in manu famuli sui, regis Francorum subegit, ut ab obsequio ejus non possit amplius separari."—p. 48.

[177] Many difficult points arose. Did Becket demand not merely the actual possessions of the see, but all to which he laid claim? There were three estates held by William de Ros, Henry of Essex, and John the Marshall (the original object of dispute at Northampton?), which Becket specifically required and declared that he would not give up if exiled for ever.—Epist. Giles, iii. 220; Bouquet, 400.

[178] Epist. Giles, iii. 262; Bouquet, 199.

[179] Epist. ibid.; Radulph de Diceto.

[180] According to Pope Alexander, Henry offered that his son should give the kiss of peace in his stead.—Giles, iv. 55.

[181] See his letter to his emissaries at Rome.—Giles, iii. 219; Bouquet, 401.

[182] Ricardus Dorubernensis apud Twysden. Lord Lyttelton has another copy, in his appendix; in that a ninth article forbade the payment of Peter's Pence to Rome; it was to be collected and brought into the exchequer.

[183] Epist. Giles, iii. 195; Bouquet, 404.

[184] Giles, iii. 192; Bouquet, 405.

[185] Dated February 12, 1170.

[186] Epist. Giles, iii. 96; Bouquet, 416; Giles, iii. 108; Bouquet, 419. "Sed pro eâ mori parati sumus." He adds: "Insurgant qui voluerint cardinales, arment non modo regem Angliæ, sed totum, si possent orbem in perniciem nostram.... Utinam via Romana non gratis peremisset tot miseros innocentes. Quis de cetero audebit illi regi registere quem ecclesia Romana tot triumphis animavit, et armavit exemplo pernitioso manante ad posteros."

[187] "Nec persuadebitur mundo, quod suasores isti Deum saperent; sed potius pecuniam, quam immoderato avaritiæ ardore sitiunt, olfecerunt."—Giles, iv. 291; Bouquet, 417.

[188] Becket's depression at this event is dwelt upon in a letter of Peter of Blois to John of Salisbury. Peter traveled from Rome to Bologna with the Papal legates. From them he gathered that either Becket would soon be reconciled to the King or be removed to another patriarchate.—Epist. xxii. apud Giles, i. p. 84.

[189] Dr. Lingard holds this letter, printed by Lord Lyttelton, and which he admits was produced, to have been a forgery. If it was, it was a most audacious one; and a most flagrant insult to the Pope, whom Henry was even now endeavoring to propitiate through the Lombard Republics and the Emperor of the East (see Giles, iv. 10). It is remarkable, too, that though the Pope declares that this coronation, contrary to his prohibition (Giles, iv. 30), is not to be taken as a precedent, he has no word of the forgery. Nor do I find any contemporary assertion of its spuriousness. Becket, indeed, in his account of the last interview with the King, only mentions the general permission granted by the Pope at an early period of the reign; and argues as if this were the only permission. Is it possible that a special permission to York to act was craftily interpolated into the general permission? But the trick may have been on the side of the Pope, now granting, now nullifying his own grants by inhibition. Bouquet is strong against Baronius (as on other points) upon Alexander's duplicity.—p. 434.

[190] Giles, iii. 229.

[191] Giles, iii. 302.

[192] "Dictum fuit aliquem dixisse vel scripsisse regi Anglorum de Archepiscopo ut quid tenetur exclusus? melius tenebitur inclusus quam exclusus. Satisque dictum fuit intelligenti."—p. 272.

[193] Giles, iv. 30; Bouquet, 436.

[194] "Nam de consuetudinibus quas tanta pervicaciâ vindicare consueverat nec mutire præsumpsit." Becket was as mute. The issue of the quarrel seems entirely changed. The Constitutions of Clarendon recede, the right of coronation occupies the chief place.—See the long letter, Giles, 65.

[195] Humbold Bishop of Ostia advised the confining the triumph to the depression of the Archbishop of York and the excommunication of the Bishops.—Giles, vi. 129; Bouquet, 443.

[196] "Licet ei (regi sc.) peperceritis, dissimulare non audetis excessus et crimina sacerdotum." This letter is a curious revelation of the arrogance and subtlety of Becket.—Giles, iii. 77.

[197] It is called the Pax.

[198] Becket disclaims vengeance: "Neque hoc dicimus, Deo teste, vindictam expetentes, quum scriptum esse noverimus, non quæres ultionem ... sed ut ecclesia correctionis exemplo possit per Dei gratiam in posterum roborare, et pœna paucorum multos ædificare."—Giles, iii. 76.

[199] See Becket's account.—Giles, iii. p. 81.

[200] Lambeth says: "Visum est autem nonnullis, quod incircumspectè literarum vindictâ post pacem usus est, que *tantum pacis desperatione fuerint datæ*"—p. 116. Compare pp. 119 and 152.

[201] Lord Lyttelton has drawn an inference from these words unfavorable to the purity of Idonea's former life; and certainly the examples of the Magdalene and the woman of Egypt, if this be not the case, were unhappily chosen.

[202] Fitz-Stephen, pp. 281, 284.

[203] Becket calls York his ancient enemy: "Lucifer ponens sedem suum in aquilone."

[204] Becket accuses the bishops of thirsting for his blood! "Let them drink it." But this was a phrase which he uses on all occasions, even to William of Pavia.

[205] "Si vero ita eidem Archiepiscopo et Cantuarensi Ecclesiæ satisfacere inveniretis, ut pœnam istam ipse videat relaxandam, vice nostrâ per illum volumus adimpleri."—Apud Bouquet, p. 461.

[206] "Ipse tamen Londonias adiens, et ibi missarum solenniis celebratis, quosdam excommunicavit."—Passio, iii. p. 154.

[207] Since this passage was written an excellent and elaborate paper has appeared in the Quarterly Review, full of local knowledge. I recognize the hand of a friend from whom great things may be expected. I find, I think, nothing in which we disagree, though that account, having more ample space, is more particular than mine. (Reprinted in Memorials of Canterbury, by Rev. A. P. Stanley.)

[208] Fitz-Stephen, De Bosham, Grim, *in loc.*

[209] See, on the former history of these knights, Quarterly Review, vol. xciii. p. 355. The writer has industriously traced out all that can be known, much which was rumored about these men.

[210] Tuesday, Dec. 29. See, on the fatality of Tuesday in Becket's life, Q. R. p. 357.

[211] Grim, p. 71. Fitz-Stephen.

[212] For the accurate local description, see Quarterly Review, p. 367.

[213] Grim, 70.

[214] John of Salisbury. Bouquet, 619, 620.

[215] Giles, iv. 162; Bouquet, 467. It was fitting that the day after that of the Holy Innocents should be that on which should rise up this new Herod.

[216] See the letter of Arnulf of Lisieux.—Bouquet, 469.

[217] The Quarterly reviewer has the merit of tracing out the extraordinary fate of the murderers. "By a singular reciprocity, the principle for which Becket had contended, that priests should not be subjected to the secular courts, prevented the trial of a layman for the murder of a priest by any other than a clerical tribunal." Legend imposes upon them dark and romantic acts of penance; history finds them in high places of trust and honor.—pp. 377, *et seqq*. I may add that John of Oxford five years after was Bishop of Norwich. Ridel too became of Ely.

[218] Diceto, p. 557.

[219] This stipulation, in Henry's view, canceled hardly any; as few, and these but trifling customs, had been admitted during his reign.

[220] The scene is related by all the monkish chroniclers.—Gervaise, Diceto, Brompton, Hoveden.

[221] Peter of Blois was assured by the two cardinal legates of Henry's innocence of Becket's death. See this letter, which contains a most high-flown eulogy on the transcendent virtues of Henry.—Epist. 66.

[222] On the effect of the death, and the immediate concourse of the people to Canterbury, Lambeth, p. 133.

[223] Herbert de Bosham, writing fourteen years after Becket's death, declares him among the most undisputed martyrs. "Quod alicujus martyrum causa justior fuit aut apertior ego nec audivi, nec legi." So completely were clerical immunities part and parcel of Christianity.

[224] The enemies of Becket assigned base reasons for his opposition to the King. "Ecclesiasticam etiam libertatem, quam defensatis, non ad animarum lucrum sed ad augmentum pecuniarum, episcopos vestros intorquere." See the charges urged by John of Oxford.—Giles, iv. p. 188.

[225] Especially in Epist. 19. "Interim."

[226] It is not just to judge the clergy by the crimes of individual men, but there is one case, mentioned by no less an authority than John of

Salisbury, too flagrant to pass over: it was in Becket's own cathedral city. Immediately after Becket's death the Bishops of Exeter and Worcester were commissioned by Pope Alexander to visit St. Augustine's, Canterbury. They report the total dilapidation of the buildings and estates. The prior elect "Jugi, quod hereticus damnat, fluit libidine, et hinnit in fœminas, adeo impudens ut libidinem, nisi quam publicaverit, voluptuosam esse non reputat." He debauched mothers and daughters: "Fornicationis abusum comparat necessitati." In one village he had seventeen bastards.—Epist. 310.

CPSIA information can be obtained
at www.ICGtesting.com
Printed in the USA
LVHW041016020323
740706LV00008B/1032

9 789356 899490